Once Bitten

A farce in three acts

adapted from Alfred Hennequin
and Alfred Delacour's *Le Procès Veauradieux*
(The Veauradieux Case)

by Reggie Oliver

Samuel French — London
www.samuelfrench-london.co.uk

ONCE BITTEN

First presented at the Orange Tree Theatre, Richmond, on 15th December 2010 with the following cast:

Fauvinard	David Antrobus
Fanchette	Amy Neilson Smith
Tardivaut	Mark Frost
Madame Laiguisier	Briony McRoberts
Angèle	Mia Austen
Thérèse	Caitlin Shannon
Gatinet	Richard Durden
Madame de Bagnolles	Rebecca Egan
Sophie	Amy Neilson Smith
Césarine	Beth Cordingley
De Bagnolles	Damien Matthews
Commissioner of Police	Michael Kirk

Directed by Sam Walters
Designed by Sam Dowson
Lighting design by John Harris
Deputy Stage Manager and sound effects: Sophie Acreman

CHARACTERS

Fauvinard, a lawyer in his 30s
Fanchette, his maid
Tardivaut, a lawyer, slightly older than Fauvinard
Madame Laiguisier, middle-aged, formidable
but not unattractive
Angèle, Fauvinard's wife
Thérèse, Fauvinard's cook
Gatinet, a dissolute-looking, elderly gentleman
Madame de Bagnolles, 30s, veiled, fashionably
dressed
Sophie, a maid, cousin of Thérèse
Césarine, a glamorous young woman
De Bagnolles, a serious man in his 30s
Commissioner of Police

SYNOPSIS OF SCENES

The action of the play takes place in two locations in
Paris

ACT I
Fauvinard's study, afternoon

ACT II
11 Rue Saint-Lazare, that night.

ACT III
Fauvinard's study, the following morning

Time — Spring, 1875

This play is dedicated to

Sam Walters MBE

and the Orange Tree Theatre

ACT I

Fauvinard's study, Spring 1875, afternoon

There are three entrances: Entrance 1 to a front door, Entrance 2 to other rooms and Entrance 3 to Fauvinard's dressing room. There is a desk piled high with documents, legal tomes etc. There is a chair behind the desk and in front of it, a sofa and a side table on which is a clock

Fauvinard, a lawyer in his 30s, is at his desk rather aimlessly shuffling papers. He wears a prominent pair of whiskers. He leans back in his chair and stares at the ceiling. There is a knock at the door. Immediately he resumes his air of business, shuffling papers etc.

Fauvinard Come in!

Fanchette, the maid, enters Entrance 1

Fanchette It's Monsieur —— Oh ...
Fauvinard Who?
Fanchette Sorry, monsieur. I forgot his name ...
Fauvinard Well, go and ask who it is.

Fanchette goes

Servants! They're getting stupider by the day.

Fanchette enters

Fanchette I remember now, monsieur. It's the lawyer.
Fauvinard Well, that narrows the field. A colleague. (*Slight pause; wearily*) Just show him in.

Tardivaut enters, also a lawyer, slightly older than Fauvinard. He carries a barrister's gown over one arm

Tardivaut!
Tardivaut Is Counsellor Fauvinard at home by any chance?

They both laugh heartily at this. Fauvinard rises and they shake hands across the desk. Fanchette joins in the laughter. Fauvinard looks at her sternly

Fauvinard That will be all, Jacques!

Tardivaut Jacques?

Fanchette My name is Fanchette, monsieur. Fanchette Beaudru. I come from ——

Fauvinard (*firmly*) No, it is Jacques! (*To Tardivaut*) It's my mother-in-law, you see.

Tardivaut Jacques is your mother-in-law?

Fauvinard No, No! My mother-in-law is called something completely different. But you see we had this servant called Jacques. And my mother-in-law sacked him.

Tardivaut This is Jacques?

Fauvinard That's right. So I said to her — my mother-in-law — I said to her very firmly. "This can't go on. Sacking people all over the place in my own home. I can't have this chopping and changing. I want Jacques back." She could see I meant business, so we compromised. My mother-in-law hired someone else — er — Fanchette, or whatever — and I still call her Jacques.

Tardivaut I see! Excellent.

Fauvinard Yes. We lawyers, you know. We have a talent for this kind of arbitration.

Tardivaut Very impressive.

Fauvinard Yes. Well ... That will be all, Jacques!

Fanchette Would you like me to warn madame?

Fauvinard Madame? Which madame?

Fanchette Madame your wife.

Fauvinard Yes, my wife, madame. Not the other er ... What d'you mean, warn her?

Fanchette About monsieur ... The lawyer.

Fauvinard Do you mean Counsellor Tardivaut?

Fanchette That one. Yes.

Fauvinard And why should you want to warn her?

Fanchette In case she wanted to see monsieur ... the lawyer.

Fauvinard Certainly not! If my wife wishes to see a lawyer she can see me. In fact you can tell her that we are not to be disturbed. We have some very important — affairs to discuss. (*He winks and smirks at Tardivaut*)

Tardivaut Legal affairs. (*He winks and smirks back*)

Fauvinard Quite so! That will be all, Jacques!

Fanchette Right you are, monsieur. (*She curtsies to Tardivaut*) Monsieur.

Fanchette goes

Fauvinard My dear Tardivaut, you've come just in time. Another five minutes and I'd have been out.
Tardivaut Where?
Fauvinard Seeing you. Or rather not seeing you. Because you would have been here seeing me, but not seeing me, because I would have been out, not seeing you here. And vice versa. So we wouldn't have seen each other.
Tardivaut Very well put.
Fauvinard Ah, you see, we lawyers have a knack for that sort of thing, don't we? Now then, what have you come to see me about? A case perhaps?
Tardivaut As a matter of fact, it's rather necessary for me to be free at nine o'clock this evening. You understand?
Fauvinard Ah, yes! Well, it so happens that it's rather necessary for me to be free at eight o'clock this evening. You follow me?
Tardivaut Well, I certainly do, don't I?
Fauvinard What ...? Oh, I see! Eight o'clock, nine o'clock. Follow you! Very amusing!

They laugh heartily

Tardivaut So that's what you wanted to see me about?
Fauvinard Yes. I was going to ask you to write me a letter, so that when I got it my wife would understand.
Tardivaut That you needed to be —
Fauvinard Out. Yes. On some sort of legitimate ... business.
Tardivaut Why? Does she have a suspicious mind?
Fauvinard No, but she has a very suspicious mother.
Tardivaut Say no more. My situation precisely, but without the mother-in-law. Exactly what I wanted you to do for me. Shall we write? Paper?

Fauvinard supplies paper ink and pen. They sit either side of the desk and begin to write

Fauvinard (*writing*) "My dear colleague ..."
Tardivaut ⎫
Fauvinard ⎬ (*together*) "I feel I should remind you ..."
Tardivaut "I have the honour of reminding you ..."
Fauvinard (*rewriting*) "Honour". Yes. Much better! "... of reminding you ... That it is tonight at — " What time did you say?

Tardivaut Nine o'clock.

Fauvinard Ah, well, now, I'm eight o'clock. The early bird, you know! (*He laughs*)

Tardivaut does not respond

Never mind. "... to remind you that we have a —— " Now what shall we say — a discussion? Arbitration?

Tardivaut Consultation.

Fauvinard Consultation! Excellent! (*Writing*) "That we have a consultation ... On the ..." Er ... Something ... Case. What shall we call it?

Tardivaut The ... Veauradieux Case.

Fauvinard The Veauradieux Case? What's that?

Tardivaut I don't know. I heard it somewhere. But it sounds very...

Fauvinard Yes, it does doesn't it? Excellent!

Tardivaut ⎱ (*together, writing*) " ... the Veauradieux Case."
Fauvinard ⎰

Tardivaut I've just had a thought. We'll need to have something to eat before we ... er ...

Fauvinard Yes. Quite!

Tardivaut Why not Bignon's?

Fauvinard Splendid! I was going to have to have dinner with my mother-in-law tonight.

Tardivaut That wouldn't have been correct. To have to have dinner with one's mother-in-law before ...

Fauvinard Precisely. Most improper!

Tardivaut Allow me to dictate.

They write

"It is therefore necessary that we should discuss this affair ... Er, case. I will be happy if you could give me the benefit of your valuable ..." um ——

Fauvinard "Expertise ..."

Tardivaut "Expertise over dinner this evening at seven o'clock precisely."

Fauvinard ⎱ (*together*) "I remain, monsieur, most respectfully yours et
Tardivaut ⎰   cetera ... et cetera ..."

Tardivaut Envelope?

Fauvinard supplies the envelopes. During the following they are putting the letters in the envelopes, writing addresses etc.

Fauvinard Now, where shall we meet?
Tardivaut Well, we'll need to have a drink before dinner, won't we?
Fauvinard But of course!
Tardivaut So shall we say the Café Helder at six? The absinthe hour.
Fauvinard Very good idea. (*Writing*) The address: "Monsieur Tardivaut, advocate ..."
Tardivaut (*writing*) "Monsieur Fauvinard, advocate ..." Stamp?

Fauvinard supplies stamps which they apply

Your letter, please!

Fauvinard hands him his letter

I'll put them in the post.
Fauvinard And we should get them by five. Splendid. (*Shaking hands warmly with Tardivaut*) My dear Tardivaut.
Tardivaut My esteemed colleague Fauvinard! You know it's funny. I'd always thought of you as so respectable.
Fauvinard Oh, but I am! My wife Angèle is a most charming woman. I love her very much.
Tardivaut Of course! Whenever a man is caught *in flagrante* with another woman he always protests that he adores his wife.
Fauvinard There you are! It's a well-known fact. Infidelity makes the heart grow fonder.
Tardivaut Well, in a way. A husband may not cheat on his wife because he adores her; but he may come to adore the lady once he's cheated on her.
Fauvinard No. I don't understand that.
Tardivaut Anyway, as you say, you love your wife, but ——
Fauvinard Angèle is an angel. She came to me with a large fortune too. Unfortunately she also came with a mother.
Tardivaut So *she* is the fly in the ointment.
Fauvinard More of a bull in a china shop.
Tardivaut Don't you mean cow?
Fauvinard My dear Tardivaut, please! Language!
Tardivaut I beg your pardon.
Fauvinard It's all her fault. You haven't got a mother-in-law, so you have absolutely no excuse for your conduct. It's different for me. If you knew her ... She is the most irritating woman imaginable. She's always after me.
Tardivaut Does she live with you?

Fauvinard No, but she might just as well. Always here, morning, noon and night. As soon as I go out she's rummaging through my papers, even in my pockets. When I'm in my study she drops in like some sort of great bomb, under the pretext that she's looking for her gloves, her handkerchief. In reality she just wants to know who I'm with, what I'm saying, what I'm up to ...

Laiguisier (*off*) Fauvinard!

Fauvinard Quiet! Here she is!

Madame Laiguisier enters, a formidable but not unattractive middle-aged woman

Laiguisier Ah, there you are! Have you seen my umbrella? (*She goes straight to Fauvinard's desk and starts rummaging through the books and papers there*)

Fauvinard It's not likely to be on my desk, is it?

Laiguisier How do I know until I've looked? (*She picks up a piece of paper. Examining it*) What's this?

Fauvinard (*snatching it back*) Well, it's not an umbrella is it, madame?

Laiguisier I know that. I'm not an imbecile. That's why I asked you what it was. (*Seeing Tardivaut*) And who is this?

Fauvinard A colleague.

Laiguisier Oh! (*Quietly to Fauvinard digging him in the ribs*) Introduce us.

Fauvinard What?

Laiguisier (*quietly but insistently to Fauvinard, digging him in the ribs*) Introduce us!

Fauvinard Oh, very well! Counsellor Tardivaut, my colleague, Madame Laiguisier, my mother-in-law.

Tardivaut Charmed, madame. (*He kisses her hand*)

Laiguisier (*coquettishly*) I do beg your pardon, Monsieur Tardivaut, but I seem to have mislaid my umbrella. So silly of me.

Tardivaut Not at all, madame.

Laiguisier Oh! Goodness me! What an empty-headed little thing I am! I remember now! I left it in the hall. Delighted to have met you, Monsieur Tardivaut.

Tardivaut (*bowing*) My pleasure entirely, madame.

Laiguisier (*as she goes, aside to Fauvinard with disapproval*) He's very cheerful for a lawyer, isn't he?

Fauvinard I can't help that, can I?

Laiguisier Did I say you could? (*She goes to the door, then to Tardivaut, smiling*) Monsieur!

Tardivaut Madame!

Laiguisier goes

Fauvinard (*shutting the door, still holding the piece of paper he snatched from her*) What a nightmare that woman is! You see! Every day it's the same. She'll end by turning me against my own wife. I'm sure she already suspects me of being unfaithful, and she hasn't a scrap of evidence.

Tardivaut What about that piece of paper?

Fauvinard Oh, that! It's just a bill. For a bracelet.

Tardivaut Jewellery? for your wife.

Fauvinard Not exactly. Occasionally she sends a bill for me to pay. Just to remind me what I owe her.

Tardivaut Her?

Fauvinard coughs

Oh, I see. For jewellery?

Fauvinard Always.

Tardivaut Same here. Just to remind me. Except with me it's music lessons. She's at the Conservatoire, you know.

Fauvinard What is she studying?

Tardivaut Everything, to judge by the bills. Oboe, viola, bassoon. Here, look! (*He produces a bill from his pocket and hands it to Fauvinard*)

Fauvinard (*reading*) "Piccolo lessons".

Tardivaut (*snatching it back*) Yes, well, that's just an example. More often than not it's the double-bass.

Fauvinard (*snatching it back*) Wait a minute! (*Reading*) The address on the top. It's Rue Saint-Lazare, number ——

Tardivaut Eleven, as it happens. Why?

Fauvinard Number eleven Rue Saint-Lazare! That's the same as mine! This is appalling!

Tardivaut You at eight, me at nine!

Fauvinard How dare you — Wait! Which floor?

Tardivaut Second.

Fauvinard Thank heaven for that! I'm on the first.

Tardivaut You're below me. What a relief! Mind you, she could be on two floors. Hair colour?

Fauvinard Blonde.

Tardivaut Thank God for that!! Mine's brunette. How did you meet?

Fauvinard Oh, chance. It wasn't as if I was on the lookout or anything. I was on an omnibus. Pure chance.

Tardivaut My dear Fauvinard, in these cases chance is very seldom pure.

Fauvinard I'm shy, you know. But by a stroke of sheer luck, I sat on her little poodle.

Tardivaut On her poodle? In an omnibus?

Fauvinard Yes, you see it was raining in the Champs-Elysées. I was out in the Champs-Elysées, in the rain. There was an omnibus passing, so I hopped on. Standing room only. The omnibus was swaying about. I lost my balance and I fell over on to this girl's muff.

Tardivaut I thought you said it was a poodle.

Fauvinard Yes. It was. But the poodle was in the muff, you see.

Tardivaut Did you kill it?

Fauvinard No. But she was very upset.

Tardivaut The girl, or the poodle?

Fauvinard Both. I was lucky not to get bitten. By either. The poodle's called Niniche. The girl's called Césarine. They made a tremendous fuss, so the conductor threw us off, all three of us: me, the girl and the poodle. Very unfair. Anyway, the girl wouldn't speak to me, but she hailed a passing cab and I heard her give the address.

Tardivaut Eleven Rue Saint-Lazare.

Fauvinard So naturally I found a vet and went round there. The vet looked at the poodle and said it was just a sprain, but naturally I had to go there the next day and see how it was.

Tardivaut And how was it?

Fauvinard Delightful. No mother-in-law. Just me, the girl and the poodle. Mind you, I could have done without the poodle. It has a loud yap and a nasty nip.

Tardivaut Funny. With me it was a duck.

Fauvinard A duck?

Tardivaut Or rather two ducks. It was in the Botanical Gardens. I saw this girl walking along with an old gentleman. Her protector, I suppose. Sweet little thing, she was. I was watching her. And she took a great shine to these ducks on the pond. Chinese ducks, you know, with the fancy coloured plumage.

Fauvinard I know the ones.

Tardivaut So I bought a couple for her. Two hundred and fifty francs they cost me. But by the time I'd bought them off the park keeper, and had a duck safely tucked under each arm, the girl and the old man had left the pond. Luckily I spotted them again. I ran after them with my ducks and arrived just in time to see them getting into a cab. Luckily I heard the old man giving the address to the driver.

Fauvinard Eleven Rue Saint-Lazare?

Tardivaut Exactly. So I put the ducks in a box and sent them round to
her with a note. She was delighted. Invited me to dinner the following
evening.
Fauvinard What did you have?
Tardivaut Roast ducks.
Fauvinard *The* roast ducks?
Tardivaut Most expensive duck I've ever had. Still, it was worth it for
the pudding afterwards. (*He looks at his watch*) Good Lord, is that the
time? I must get to the post or we won't have our letters in time.
Fauvinard Till this evening, then. Six o'clock.
Tardivaut Café Helder.

Tardivaut goes off Entrance 1

(*Off*) Good-afternoon, madame!
Laiguisier (*off*) Ah, Monsieur Tardivaut!
Tardivaut (*off*) Excuse me, madame.
Fauvinard Good God! Her again! Is there no peace in this house!

Fauvinard goes off Entrance 3

The front door slams

Laiguisier (*off*) Goodbye, Monsieur Tardivaut! Most extraordinary!

Laiguisier enters with Angèle

Fauvinard! Not here. Most extraordinary!
Angèle Armand must have gone out.
Laiguisier He's always out. It's a bad sign. You must talk to him,
Angèle.
Angèle Yes, Mother.
Laiguisier Be firm.
Angèle Yes, Mother.
Laiguisier Don't give in.
Angèle No, Mother.
Laiguisier I know men. Paris has the worst possible effect on men like
Fauvinard. He is a lawyer, but he has no work, no cases. He'll ruin
himself. He'll ruin you. We'll all be ruined.
Angèle Oh, Mother, you're frightening me.
Laiguisier He must leave Paris. He could become a local magistrate or
something. If only he had clients, but he hasn't. And it's no use leaving
his lamp on half the night in his study pretending he's got work to

do. He hasn't. Well, goodbye, my dear, and don't forget you're both dining with me tonight.

Angèle No, Mother.

Laiguisier goes off Entrance 1. Fauvinard puts his head round the door Entrance 3

Fauvinard Has she gone? (*He enters the room, half in evening dress, still adjusting his tie etc.*)

Angèle You were here all the time. Why didn't you come and say goodbye to Mother?

Fauvinard Angèle, my dear, you know I'd love to say goodbye to your mother.

Angèle Oh, Armand! That's not very kind.

Fauvinard I mean I'd said good-morning to her. I even embraced her. One can have too much of a good thing.

Angèle She's very fond of you, you know. She's always talking about you.

Fauvinard In the wrong hands I can be a very tedious topic of conversation.

Angèle (*sitting on the sofa and beckoning him to sit next to her*) Come and sit next to me. I want to talk about an idea we had this morning.

Fauvinard We? What idea is this? (*He sits next to Angèle*)

Angèle (*adjusting his tie, brushing his lapel etc.*) You know La Rénaudière?

Fauvinard Your mother's property near Orléans. Yes, of course I know it.

Angèle The people there are charming.

Fauvinard Hilarious. The priest, the vet, the deputy mayor. One's spoilt for exciting company.

Angèle And whist nearly every evening.

Fauvinard I know, I know. It's a continuous round of gaiety, and one goes to bed at nine, just like the hens. It's a sort of healthy grave.

Angèle So why don't we go and live there?

Fauvinard And leave Paris?

Angèle Why not?

Fauvinard Well, it's an idea. One of your mother's no doubt?

Angèle There's a position of Justice of the Peace going, and Mother says she's sure she can get it for you.

Fauvinard Will you thank your mother but I am not interested in anything she can offer me. I have a career to think of.

Angèle It's so expensive here. And you know what mother says: "Paris finds mischief for idle men to do."

Fauvinard I am not idle. I am a barrister, a lawyer.
Angèle But you haven't had a case. Two years we've been married and
no briefs. Not a single one.
Fauvinard They'll come. Every day I go to the Palais de Justice. I wear
my robe. I walk up and down. I make myself known.
Angèle That's all very well ——
Fauvinard My dear Angèle, you mustn't worry your pretty little head
about such things. You see, I am a Parisian. It's in my blood. I can't
live in some hole in the provinces. In Paris it takes time to make your
mark.
Angèle If only you had a case. Even if it was only a criminal one, Mother
would be so pleased. You know how fascinated she is by criminals.
Fauvinard I'm sure it's mutual.
Angèle Just one case ...
Fauvinard Well, only today a colleague and I were discussing a case.
Angèle Only discussing?
Fauvinard But something may come of it. In fact I'm expecting any
moment to hear from him.
Angèle What case?
Fauvinard The ... Veauradieux Case.
Angèle The Veauradieux Case!
Fauvinard (*alarmed*) You've heard about it?
Angèle Yes. But just the name. What's it about?
Fauvinard Well, it's a very complicated affair. I don't want to go into
it now.
Angèle I think I heard Mother mention it.
Fauvinard Ah, I see. Well, I'd rather you didn't say anything about it
to her ... I want it to be a surprise ... if it comes off.
Angèle If what comes off?
Fauvinard That's the surprise.
Laiguisier (*off*) How dare you! Will you be quiet!
Angèle Mother!
Fauvinard Still here!

Laiguisier enters through Entrance 2

Laiguisier Insolent young woman! Insolent young woman!
Fauvinard What is it, madame?
Laiguisier Fauvinard, I would be obliged if you would show your cook
the door. This instant!
Fauvinard Not again!
Angèle What's happened?

Laiguisier I was just on my way out when I said to myself, I'll just go and cast an eye over the kitchen. Thérèse was not there. She seldom is.

Fauvinard She must have gone out.

Laiguisier (*pointedly*) Some people have a habit of being out. So, I thought I would conduct a thorough inspection. And do you know what I found? A letter in one of the saucepans. I had just begun to read it when she came in and ——

Thérèse enters through Entrance 2, having been listening at the door

Thérèse And what right had you to read private letters?

Laiguisier What are you doing here? How dare you listen at the keyhole?

Angèle Leave us, Thérèse.

Laiguisier Anyway it wasn't your letter, Thérèse.

Thérèse I never said it was.

Fauvinard Then whose was it?

Laiguisier (*to Fauvinard*) It was addressed to you, Fauvinard.

Fauvinard What!

Thérèse There you are!

Laiguisier Then what was it doing in your saucepan?

Thérèse It had just arrived. Fanchette gave it to me but she had to go out so I was going to bring it up to monsieur, but then I had to go out and I forgot. And what right had you to read monsieur's letter?

Fauvinard Exactly!

Laiguisier (*to Fauvinard*) Be quiet! (*To Thérèse*) How dare you! Leave the room this instant!

Thérèse goes, but remains behind the door

Fauvinard Now then, what's all this about a letter of mine?

Laiguisier Ah, yes, I was going to ask you about that.

Fauvinard You ask me about my private correspondence, madame?

Laiguisier (*removing the paper from her corsage*) Doesn't look very private to me. It seems to be some sort of receipt for some jewellery.

Angèle Jewellery?

Fauvinard What? Oh! Yes! Let me see! (*He snatches it from Laiguisier. He looks at it*) Ah, yes, of course!

Laiguisier What?

Fauvinard It's to do with ... A case I'm working on. With my colleague Tardivaut. You met him just now.

Laiguisier Then what's he doing sending you messages when you've just seen him?

Fauvinard He didn't. This is evidence.
Laiguisier You never told me you had a case.
Fauvinard It's very confidential.
Angèle The Veauradieux Case!
Fauvinard (*to Angèle*) Shh!
Angèle I'm so sorry, Armand!
Fauvinard It's very confidential. (*He puts the paper on his desk*)
Laiguisier The Veauradieux Case! Ah, yes! I was talking about that only
the other day. Do you remember Angèle? Now, what was I saying?
Fauvinard (*hastily*) Well, never mind about that now! Let's get back to
the matter in hand. This business with Thérèse.
Laiguisier I was just about to tell you before you interrupted me. Now
I was giving her the benefit of some helpful advice about how to do
her job properly — in a perfectly friendly way — when she muttered
something under her breath. You will not believe me when I tell you.
Angèle What was it, Mother?
Laiguisier She said — you will not believe this — she said ... (*hesitantly*)
"old boiler".
Fauvinard Old boiler! I believe you. (*He suppresses laughter with a fit
of coughing and goes to sit behind his desk*)

Thérèse appears from behind the door

Thérèse That's a dirty lie. I did not call you an old boiler.
Laiguisier Are you denying that you said "old boiler" under your
breath?
Thérèse Oh, no!
Laiguisier Well, then!
Thérèse I may have said "old boiler", but I wasn't calling you an old
boiler. I was just saying "old boiler". I was reminding myself that
we've got an old boiler and that we could do with a new one, for the
vegetables.
Laiguisier A likely story.
Thérèse I see! So you think it was more probable that I was calling you
an old boiler. I wonder why that is!
Laiguisier Impertinence. Did you hear that? Thérèse, you are dismissed.
Pack your things.
Thérèse Oh, yes! Who says? Who's the mistress in this house?
Laiguisier Angèle! Tell her who is mistress in this house!
Angèle (*meekly*) Thérèse, you are dismissed.
Thérèse (*to Angèle*) Oh, so you've dared to open your mouth have you?
(*Taking off her apron and throwing it on the sofa*) Well, you won't find
a replacement for me in a hurry.

Thérèse goes, Entrance 1

Laiguisier Servants! They're all the same.

Fauvinard I sincerely hope not. You'd be sacking them as fast as we could hire them. We now have no cook.

Laiguisier Could you have sat down to a meal prepared by a woman who had grossly insulted your wife's mother?

Fauvinard That would depend on what she had been cooking. She was rather a good cook ... as cooks go.

Laiguisier Fauvinard, you have no heart!

Fauvinard Perhaps not, but I do have a stomach.

Laiguisier (*ignoring him, to Angèle*) Now then, have you spoken to your husband?

Angèle Yes, Mother.

Laiguisier Well, then?

Fauvinard I absolutely refuse!

Laiguisier You must have some very good reasons for staying in Paris ——

Fauvinard I do ——

Laiguisier But I have yet to hear you plead your first case.

Fauvinard There is more to law than standing in front of a jury. There are consultations, arbitrations. Like this Veauradieux case for example, that I'm working on.

Laiguisier Ah, yes! I want to hear more about that.

Fauvinard It's confidential.

Laiguisier Now, what was it I was saying about the Veauradieux case only the other day?

Fauvinard (*hastily*) Yes, well any moment I am expecting my colleague Tardivaut to send me a note inviting me to dinner tonight to discuss the matter.

Laiguisier But you're dining with me!

Fauvinard Business before pleasure, I'm afraid, madame!

Laiguisier But you've only just seen Tardivaut.

Fauvinard We have a lot to discuss.

Laiguisier But if you know you're going to dine with him, why does he have to send you a note asking you?

Fauvinard Well, it's perfectly simple ... He said, "let's discuss this over dinner," so I said: "Invite me." So he said: "I'll write you a note." That's the proper thing to do. So he did. I mean he's going to. I mean, he probably has, but I don't know, do I? Why are you asking me all these questions?

Laiguisier You should have done your discussing here instead of wasting your money over dinner.

Fauvinard But we both had business to attend to, clients to see, that sort of thing.

Laiguisier Clients? What clients do you have?

Fauvinard Well ... Gatinet, for example.

Laiguisier Is he coming here?

Fauvinard He might be. I don't know, do I?

Laiguisier Anyway, he's not a client; he's your uncle.

Fauvinard I manage his affairs.

Laiguisier You bail him out when he's squandered all his money. He's a worthless old scamp, and he sets you a bad example.

Fauvinard He's very fond of you.

Laiguisier I can't help that, can I?

Fauvinard Did I say you could? That is my point. We can't help having relations. We are born with our uncles, our mothers ...

Laiguisier Oh, so you're a philosopher now. I tell you, I won't have him in this house.

Fauvinard You don't have to, but I will!

Gatinet enters through Entrance 1, a dissolute-looking, elderly gentleman

Uncle Gatinet!

Gatinet Ah! I let myself in. Someone seemed to be going out in a hurry, so I came in. (*He sees Laiguisier. His eyes light up. He goes to her, takes her hand and kisses it avidly*) Ah, madame! How delightful to see you!

Laiguisier Monsieur Gatinet!

Gatinet Ah, Fauvinard! What a lucky man you are to have such a mother-in-law. A fine figure of a woman! A fine figure of a woman!

Laiguisier (*backing away from him*) What are you doing here, Monsieur Gatinet?

Gatinet I have come to see you, madame! And I have some er ... business with my nephew. But it is for you that I long, madame!

Laiguisier (*backing away from him*) Do sit down, monsieur!

Gatinet No! I can't possibly do that! It would be fatal.

Fauvinard Why?

Gatinet Well, not exactly fatal, but ... It's a funny thing, you see, but nowadays, whenever I sit down I fall asleep. During the day that is. At night I'm fine usually. I'm often up all night. Doesn't seem to affect me. Then day comes and I have to stay standing, or — bang! — I'm out like a light. Only the other evening, I was saying to Zizi ——

Laiguisier Zizi! And who is Zizi?

Gatinet (*pursuing her round the room*) Oh, madame! Do not be offended, but ever since you rejected my suit, I have been trying to forget. This Zizi, she means nothing to me, but she ... She helps me forget you!

Laiguisier (*backing away from him*) Oh, really!

Fauvinard (*aside*) Useful girl! I should like to meet her.

Laiguisier (*backing towards the door Entrance 2*) Well, we must leave you to your affairs. Angèle, we shall discuss this cook business and find you another.

Angèle (*following her*) Yes, Mother.

Gatinet Your servant, madame!

Laiguisier I think not, monsieur.

Fauvinard I doubt if you would enjoy the experience.

Laiguisier Fauvinard, don't let this man corrupt you, if he hasn't already done so. Come, Angèle!

Laiguisier goes off Entrance 2 with Angèle

Gatinet (*following her to the door. Looking after her*) Ah, that's a fine figure of a woman. Reminds me of my mother. I think I could make her very happy.

Fauvinard Only by leaving her alone. Forget it, Uncle. Sit down.

Gatinet Oh, thank you, dear boy —— (*about to sit, then remembering himself*) No! No, I mustn't. I have a couple of things to talk to you about. The first thing ... I forget. But the second thing is, my allowance. Twenty-five thousand francs.

Fauvinard What about it?

Gatinet It's due.

Fauvinard I know it's due. I've already paid it to you.

Gatinet Oh. Have you? I don't remember. Well ... how about an advance?

Fauvinard I've already given you one of those, too.

Gatinet Have you? Oh. My memory's like a sieve. Ah! Wait a minute, I remember now!

Fauvinard You remember my giving you money?

Gatinet No, no! I remember the first thing I meant to say to you. I knew it should have come first. This'll soften him up, I said to myself. I've found you a client.

Fauvinard A client! With a case!

Gatinet First rate affair. Very rich lady — wants to chuck her husband.

Fauvinard A fashionable divorce! Splendid! This could be the making of me. (*Sitting at his desk, eagerly taking up his pen to make notes*) Now ... The lady's name.

Gatinet Madame ... Madame ... Something-or-other. I can't quite ...
(*He begins to sit down. Fauvinard dashes out from behind his desk to
prevent him from doing so*)
Fauvinard No, no! You mustn't sit down or you'll fall asleep.
Remember?
Gatinet Oh, yes! I forgot.
Fauvinard Now, this lady. Madame ...?
Gatinet Madame ... No, it's gone.
Fauvinard Well, never mind that now. How did you come across her?
Gatinet Ah, yes, well I remember that. I met her while I was paying a
call at a house in the Rue ... No, the Boulevard ... Er ...
Fauvinard Yes, well never mind that now. Go on.
Gatinet And this lady said she was looking for someone to handle her
divorce. And Zizi, she recommended someone. Spoke very highly of
him. Counsellor ... Er. No, the name's gone. It'll come back to me.
Fauvinard Never mind. Go on!
Gatinet Well, I was asked my opinion, and I had to think quickly, so I
said: "Ah! Yes. This Counsellor What's-his-name. A true ornament of
the law courts. Such a pity he has to leave Paris."
Fauvinard Why?
Gatinet I was thinking on my feet, you see. I can't do it any other way.
I told her that he had got a paralysed tongue and that the Faculty have
sent him off to Italy.
Fauvinard I see! Good grief!
Gatinet So naturally I was asked to recommend someone else and I
suggested you, dear boy. I said I knew you by reputation, that you
were a specialist in family disputes, and an expert in divorces. I said
that I knew of no less than fifty families, some of the most united
and loving in all France, which you had managed to separate by your
incomparable forensic skill. Then I gave her your address. She should
be here any minute now.
Fauvinard I am much obliged to you. Particularly for giving this
Counsellor what's-his-name paralysis of the tongue. That was
inspired.
Gatinet Thank you. Not at all. Now about my allowance ——
Fauvinard Why don't you sit down, Uncle? (*He tries to push him into
a chair*)

Gatinet avoids him

Gatinet No. No. Now about the allowance.
Fauvinard I told you. You've been paid.
Gatinet Ah. Funny, you see. I'd forgotten all about it. All I need is an
advance of say ... Ten thousand?

Fauvinard Ten thousand! What on earth do you spend it on?

Gatinet Well, you see Zizi, this little girl I'm seeing to forget your mother-in-law, she's studying at the Conservatoire. She's learning all kinds of instruments; and of course, she needs money for music lessons.

Fauvinard Music lessons! Where have I heard that before?

Gatinet She studies very hard, you know. Often I can't get to see her because someone's in there teaching her the oboe, or whatever. She has all these different teachers you see. So if you could give me a little advance in lieu of ——

Fauvinard I am not interested in your advances. I will not pay for your mistress's masters, always assuming they are her masters and she isn't their mistress as well. Now, if you will excuse me I have business to attend to.

Gatinet What about a finder's fee?

Fauvinard Sit down!

Gatinet Will you stop telling me to sit down. You know perfectly well ——

Fauvinard pushes him into a chair. Gatinet almost immediately falls asleep

Fauvinard Thank heaven for that!

Fanchette enters

Ah! Jacques! Has the post arrived?

Fanchette No, monsieur, but there's a lady here to see you.

Fauvinard What lady? What's her name?

Fanchette I didn't ask her.

Fauvinard Then why not, you fool?

Fanchette Because she asked me not to ask her. She said, "Don't ask me my name." So I didn't.

Fauvinard Ah! It's confidential. It must be the client. Show her in.

Fanchette Yes, monsieur.

Fanchette goes

Fauvinard goes to Gatinet and tries to wake him up

Fauvinard Gatinet! Gatinet! Wake up!

Gatinet (*murmuring in his sleep*) Mother!

Fauvinard lifts him up bodily and puts him on his feet

Who? What's going on?
Fauvinard She's arrived!
Gatinet Who?
Fauvinard The client you got me.

Gatinet begins to collapse. Fauvinard walks him around the room to wake him up

Now then, what's her name?
Gatinet Whose name?
Fauvinard The client.
Gatinet Which client?
Fauvinard Oh, you're useless!
Gatinet No! I remember the name now.
Fauvinard You do!
Gatinet Yes. It's Tardivaut.
Fauvinard Good God! Do you mean to say the name of this divorce client you got me is Madame Tardivaut?
Gatinet No. No! The lawyer!
Fauvinard What lawyer?
Gatinet The lawyer, this girl recommended. The one I said had got paralysis of the tongue and had to go to Italy. Counsellor Tardivaut.
Fauvinard Oh, good grief!
Gatinet Now, I know what I came to see you about. My allowance ——
Fauvinard Not now! I've got a client.
Gatinet Oh, have you? Congratulations. So perhaps you could see your way to ——
Fauvinard (*moving him to the door*) Later!
Gatinet (*as he is bundled out of the door*) I'll just go and see how your mother-in-law is getting on. Might have another pop at her. Fine figure of a woman. I'll come back later for the ten thousand ...

By this time he is out of the door

Fauvinard rushes to his desk, sits, arranges his paper and has just had time to assume a businesslike pose when ...

Fanchette enters

Fanchette Madame ... (*She coughs to cover her ignorance*)

Madame de Bagnolles enters, in her thirties, veiled, fashionably dressed

Fauvinard Ah! Madame ... (*He coughs like Fanchette. Rising and leading her to a seat with great obsequiousness*) Will you do me the honour of being seated?

Mme de B sits. Fauvinard goes to his desk and shuffles through his papers again with a great show of business

Please excuse me. I have so many clients to attend to. Hard to keep up with them all sometimes!

Mme de B There was a man just going out as I came in.

Fauvinard Ah, yes. Another case, you see.

Mme de B I thought I recognized him. I could come back later if ...

Fauvinard No, no! (*Finished with his shuffling*) Now, madame, I am at your service.

Mme de B I'll begin at the beginning, shall I?

Fauvinard Always the best place to start in my experience, madame.

Mme de B Monsieur, my parents were very rich but I had the misfortune to lose them early in life. At eighteen I became the mistress of a large fortune, but an orphan.

Fauvinard How delightful — how sad!

Mme de B I met a young man. I fell in love with him and without considering his lack of fortune, I married him. For two years Monsieur de Bagnolles was charming to me.

Fauvinard Monsieur de Bagnolles?

Mme de B My husband.

Fauvinard Oh, your husband!

Mme de B He was a superb lover.

Fauvinard This is your husband?

Mme de B Yes! Monsieur de Bagnolles.

Fauvinard Of course. Forgive me, I am unused to husbands being described as superb ... Hmm! So you are Madame de (*writing it down*) Bagnolles. Please continue.

Laiguisier enters. She fails to see Mme de B

Laiguisier (*to Fauvinard*) Ah, there you are! Have you seen my yellow gloves? (*She goes straight to Fauvinard's desk and starts rummaging through the books and papers there*)

Fauvinard They're not likely to be on my desk, are they?

Laiguisier How do I know until I've looked? (*Seeing Mme de B, suspiciously*) And who is this?

Fauvinard A client of mine.
Laiguisier (*suspiciously*) Are you sure?
Fauvinard Of course I'm sure!
Laiguisier Oh! (*Quietly to Fauvinard digging him in the ribs*) Introduce us.
Fauvinard What?
Laiguisier (*quietly but insistently to Fauvinard digging him in the ribs*) Introduce us!
Fauvinard Oh, very well! My client, Madame de Bagnolles. Madame Laiguisier, my mother-in-law.
Mme de B How do you do, madame.
Laiguisier I do beg your pardon, Madame de Bagnolles, but I seem to have mislaid my yellow gloves. So silly of me.
Mme de B Not at all, madame.
Laiguisier (*rummaging again through the books and papers on the desk, she picks up a piece of paper. Examining it*) What's this?
Fauvinard (*snatching it back*) Well, it's not your yellow gloves, is it, Madame!
Laiguisier I know that. I'm not an imbecile. Oh, I remember; it's something to do with the Veauradieux case.
Mme de B The Veauradieux case?
Fauvinard (*hastily*) Yes. Another of my cases. Now, if you will excuse us, dear mother-in-law —— (*He starts to push her towards the door*)
Laiguisier (*turning back*) Do you know about the Veauradieux case, madame?
Mme de B Well, not really, but they spoke very highly of the lawyer on the case.
Laiguisier My son-in-law here?
Mme de B No. Counsellor Tardivaut. In fact I was going to employ him ——
Laiguisier Ah, Counsellor Tardivaut! Such a charming man! (*Pointedly*) Plenty of clients.
Mme de B I was so sorry to hear about his condition.
Laiguisier What condition?
Fauvinard (*hastily*) Well, we don't want to go into all that now, do we?
Mme de B Paralysis of the tongue, I believe.
Fauvinard (*hastily, guiding Laiguisier towards the door*) Yes, very sad. An occupational hazard, I'm afraid.
Laiguisier (*turning back*) But I saw Counsellor Tardivaut only just now and ——
Fauvinard It comes and goes. His tongue became paralysed soon after you left him.

Laiguisier Really, how?

Fauvinard (*hurriedly*) Need you ask? He'd just seen you. Terrible business. (*By this time he has got her to the door*) Now, then if you have finished looking for your yellow gloves in here, madame and I have some business to attend to.

Laiguisier Oh! Goodness me! What an empty-headed little thing I am! I remember now! I left my yellow gloves in the dining room. Delighted to have met you, madame.

Mme de B My pleasure entirely, madame.

Laiguisier (*as she goes, aside to Fauvinard with disapproval*) She's very attractive for a client, isn't she?

Fauvinard I can't help that, can I?

Laiguisier Did I say you could? I've got my eye on you. (*She goes to the door, then to Mme de B, smiling*) Madame!

Mme de B Madame!

Laiguisier (*to Fauvinard*) And it's wide open!

Laiguisier goes

Fauvinard If only she were mother-in-law to one of my friends, how amusing I should find her! (*To Mme de B*) A thousand pardons, madame, for the interruption. You were saying that for the first two years Monsieur de Bagnolles was charming.

Mme de B Then he began to squander my fortune.

Fauvinard Gambling?

Mme de B Certainly not! My husband is not a gambler.

Fauvinard Ah, I see!

Mme de B He is involved with a married woman. He is a very passionate man.

Fauvinard (*rubbing his hands*) Splendid! Splendid! I mean ... oh, dear!

Mme de B And a superb lover, of course.

Fauvinard Oh, good!

Mme de B Unfortunately. This woman's husband is in England. She is completely unscrupulous.

Fauvinard Good. Good.

Mme de B She has become involved in some very shady dealings. Counsellor Barbotin is handling her affairs.

Fauvinard Of course. Of course. I know him well.

Mme de B Counsellor Barbotin is an old family friend. He warned me of the situation, of my husband's association with this woman. I wanted him to handle my case, naturally, but he said there might have been a conflict of interest. Counsellor Barbotin is a man of complete integrity.

Fauvinard Of course.

Mme de B So he simply told me exactly what sort of a woman his client was and advised me to find another lawyer.

Fauvinard Excellent! He was quite correct.

Mme de B You see, if my husband were caught with this woman, there would be a terrible scandal. That must be avoided at all costs.

Fauvinard On the contrary, madame! That is what we must endeavour to obtain.

Mme de B Oh, no!

Fauvinard Oh, yes, madame! Then your own separation from him would be easy to achieve. The means might be perhaps a little violent, but ——

Mme de B No. No! I want to save my husband from ruin. He is a passionate man, you see, a superb lover, easily led astray. That is why I went to see his mistress only yesterday, to prevent a catastrophe. But she wasn't in, so I spoke to the lady in the flat above, and her friend recommended you.

Fauvinard I see! But ——

Mme de B Never mind. The point is, I need to prevent my husband from doing any more damage. He has already spent two hundred thousand ——

Fauvinard Two hundred thousand squandered on mistresses!

Mme de B Two hundred thousand!

Fanchette enters, unseen by them

Fauvinard (*rising, hands grasping lapels, as though making a speech in court*) Mistresses! You are the lepers of the modern world, a disease in the body politic. You carry misfortune, misery and shame into the sacred precinct of the family. What words are harsh enough to excoriate you? To place you in the pillory of shame. You and your accomplices ——

Fanchette giggles

Mme de B Monsieur, we are not alone!

Fauvinard Fanchette! What are you doing here?

Fanchette There's a client to see you, monsieur.

Fauvinard Another?

Fanchette Very urgent, monsieur.

Mme de B (*rising to go*) I won't delay you any longer, monsieur.

Fauvinard (*taking her hand, solemnly*) Madame, take my advice. Let us waste no time in informing the police of your husband's conduct. Let his every movement be watched. We must catch him *in flagrante*!

Mme de B Is this really necessary?

Fauvinard Madame. Take my word for it. If you want him back, then he must first be caught! You see before you a man of the world and an experienced lawyer. A man who has looked into the iniquitous depths of a man's heart. If you delay one moment you will allow this scoundrel to squander your entire fortune on a worthless woman. You must act at once!

Mme de B (*after a slight hesitation*) Very well, monsieur. I shall. And I will have the honour of waiting on you tomorrow morning.

Fauvinard Madame, I shall be at your service. (*To Fanchette*) Show the lady out, Jacques. And show in my next client.

Fanchette and Mme de B exit

When they have gone, he loses his dignity, rubs his hands, and does a gleeful little dance

Fanchette returns and catches him at it

Well? Show in my next client.

Fanchette There isn't one, monsieur.

Fauvinard What! This is outrageous. How dare you!

Fanchette Madame, your mother-in-law sent me.

Fauvinard She did what!

Fanchette She said you were spending too long alone with that woman.

Gatinet enters followed by Laiguisier and Angèle

Fauvinard Get out! Not you! I was talking to Jacques.

Fanchette goes

Gatinet How did it go?

Fauvinard Congratulate me! I've got a divorce!

Laiguisier I beg your pardon!

Fauvinard And a big one too! A real scandal. It'll be in all the papers!

Angèle (*close to tears*) I don't understand.

Fauvinard The plaintiff beautiful, abused, rich ... The husband, charming, aristocratic, a wastrel ...

Laiguisier A wastrel certainly!

Fauvinard And I am for the plaintiff!

Laiguisier Oh, I see! This is your client.

Fauvinard That's right. Madame de Bagnolles. The lady who was here just now.
Gatinet All thanks to me! (*He sits and falls asleep*)
Fauvinard The Palais de Justice will be packed. Police cordon outside. I'll stand before the judge; I'll say: "To whom does this woman owe her misery? Her husband's mistress. Mistresses!

Fanchette enters with a letter. She endeavours to interrupt him discreetly

(*Paying no attention*) You are the lepers of the modern world, a disease in the body politic. You carry misfortune, misery and shame into the sacred precinct of the family. What —— "
Fanchette (*eventually tugging his sleeve*) Letter for you, monsieur.
Fauvinard Give it to me.
Laiguisier (*snatching it from Fanchette*) Let me see.
Fauvinard (*snatching it from Laiguisier*) My letter, I think, madame. (*Opening it, but only glancing at it*) Ah, yes, of course! The consultation! My hat and coat, Jacques!

Fanchette looks blank

Fanchette!

Fanchette goes

(*To Laiguisier*) I am afraid I shall not have the pleasure of dining with you tonight. Most regrettable. But I have important business. A consultation. About a case.
Laiguisier What case?
Fauvinard The Veauradieux Case
Laiguisier Ah, yes! I remembered something about the Veauradieux Case. I wanted to ask you ——

Fanchette enters with Fauvinard's hat, coat, gloves, stick etc.

Business of him putting these on in the ensuing dialogue

Fauvinard Yes, well, not now! (*To Fanchette trying to help him on with his coat*) Wrong arm, you imbecile!
Laiguisier (*standing between him and the door*) Who are you consulting with?
Fauvinard (*handing her the letter*) My colleague Tardivaut, if you must know. (*Pointing to the letter as evidence*) There! Satisfied?

Neither of them actually looks at the letter

Laiguisier But you said he had a paralysed tongue.
Fauvinard Who?
Laiguisier Monsieur Tardivaut.
Fauvinard What? Oh. Yes. Yes, he has! Poor fellow.
Laiguisier And you're going to consult with him ... With a paralysed
    tongue ...?
Fauvinard He needs all the help he can get.
Laiguisier Over dinner?
Fauvinard Even a fellow with a paralysed tongue must eat, madame.
    Have a heart. I can help. Cut up his *filet mignon*. That sort of thing. He
    needs me. It's a mission of mercy. Now, if you will excuse me. (*He
    starts to go*)
Laiguisier Aren't you going to kiss your wife?
Fauvinard (*absently kissing Angèle*) Oh, yes, of course. Goodbye, dear
    Angèle. Don't wait up for me. I'll have to see poor Tardivaut home.
    Put him to bed. That sort of thing. I must fly.
Laiguisier But there's something I want to ask you about the Veauradieux
    Case!
Fauvinard No time. I must go. Ask Gatinet over there. He knows all
    about it. (*He indicates the still sleeping Gatinet*) Goodbye.

Fauvinard goes

Laiguisier (*going over and trying to rouse Gatinet*) Gatinet! Gatinet!

Gatinet mumbles incoherently in his sleep

    Useless! (*She looks casually at the letter in her hand*) How very odd!
    (*She examines it more closely*)
Angèle What is it, Mother?
Laiguisier This isn't a letter from Tardivaut at all. It seems to be a
    receipt for some jewellery. And there's an address on it: "Eleven Rue
    Saint-Lazare"!
Angèle What does that mean, Mother?
Laiguisier (*shouting*) Fauvinard! Come back!

Fanchette enters with a letter

    Ah, Fanchette, where is your master?
Fanchette Gone out, madame. And this letter's just arrived for him.
Laiguisier (*snatching it from her*) Give it to me. (*She opens it and reads
    it standing over Gatinet*)

Gatinet is still asleep

This one is from Tardivaut. (*Reading*) "My dear colleague ... Have the honour of reminding you ... The Veauradieux Case" Of course! The Veauradieux Case! I remember now. Do you recall those sensational jewel robberies in the Rue Saint-Honoré?

Angèle Yes, Mother.

Laiguisier That's the Veauradieux Case! The man accused was one Antoine Veauradieux, a most disreputable man. He has fled abroad, but the police are in hot pursuit. But it is believed he has an accomplice still in Paris. This jewellery receipt could secure his conviction — or the opposite! It could be a vital clue! Angèle, we must help your husband and poor Counsellor Tardivaut with their new case.

Angèle Yes, Mother.

Laiguisier You shall dine with me, then you come back here in a cab. Meanwhile I shall go to this address and see what I can find out about the Veauradieux Case. Do you understand, Angèle?

Angèle Yes, Mother!

Gatinet wakes up and sees Laiguisier looming over him. He tries to struggle to his feet

Gatinet Mother! Mother!

Laiguisier Oh, go back to sleep! (*She pushes him back into a chair*)

Gatinet falls asleep again

Eleven Rue Saint-Lazare!

Quick fade to black-out

END OF ACT I

ACT II

11 Rue Saint-Lazare, that night

There are four entrances, Entrance 1 giving on to the hallway and the entrance to the apartment, Entrance 2 to the bedroom, Entrance 3 to another room and Entrance 4 to a corridor leading to kitchen, servants' quarters, back service stairs etc. There is a chaise-longue and an upright piano on which is a lamp. On an easel there is a framed picture of a black poodle. There is an armchair and a largish round table with a heavy velvet tablecloth reaching to the floor. There is a pack of cards on the table. A small escritoire is in one corner. Generally the furnishings are more colourful and exotic than the first act

Thérèse is standing rather uncertainly in the middle of the room, her cousin Sophie, the maid, is with her

We hear the barking of a dog, small but obviously very aggressive

Césarine (*off*) Niniche! No! Naughty dog! Be quiet!

Césarine enters from Entrance 2, a glamorous young woman in a colourful loose gown or negligée. She carries a letter

She'll have to go. She really is impossible these days. So, tell me, Thérèse, why did you leave?
Thérèse She called me an old boiler.
Cesarine Your mistress?
Thérèse Her mother.
Césarine Huh! Always the way!
Sophie She is so common that woman, madame. I keep telling Cousin Thérèse. You mustn't keep working for these common people.
Césarine And what am I supposed to do about it?
Sophie If my cousin could stay here for a while, Madame Césarine. I'm sure she'll give satisfaction.
Césarine Well, you can stay here for the time being, I suppose. (*She sits at the table, studying the letter*)
Sophie Madame is so kind. (*Prompting Thérèse*) Thank madame!
Thérèse I am most grateful, madame.

Césarine (*reading the letter*) The kitchen is through there. (*She indicates Entrance 4*)
Thérèse Good-night, madame.
Césarine Good-night.

Thérèse exits via Entrance 4

Sophie Is Madame expecting anyone this evening?
Césarine Only Monsieur D'Erignac. I'll receive him in here. And will you make sure that Niniche is kept firmly shut up in there? (*She indicates Entrance 2*) Ever since that accident in the omnibus, she's taken to biting the visitors. It's not good for business. (*She looks again at the letter*)
Sophie No, madame. (*Slight pause*) You look upset, madame.
Césarine I am, Sophie. It's this letter from England.
Sophie From madame's husband?
Césarine Yes. Antoine.

In the ensuing she puts down the letter, picks up the cards and, after shuffling, deals ten of them on to the table face down. During the next she then slowly turns the cards face upwards, the last of them being the Queen of Spades

He's threatening to come back ...
Sophie But I thought —— !
Césarine Of course, it would be madness! The police are still after him. I don't think he trusts me.
Sophie But madame has done exactly what he wanted.
Césarine Yes. I have managed to obtain valid receipts for nearly all the jewellery that he has — has in his possession, so that when he sells it, everything can appear entirely legitimate and above board. I have not told him exactly how I obtained those receipts ——
Sophie Madame bought other items of jewellery and ——
Césarine Or had them bought for me and with them the receipts. But now he has become suspicious. Why are all men so suspicious, Sophie?
Sophie Because they're not clever enough to know us, madame. They can only suspect.
Césarine Very true. You should go far, Sophie. And when all this is over, that is just what I will advise you to do. Everything was going so well. Everyone was being so obliging, and now Antoine is threatening to come back to Paris and spoil everything! (*Turning up the Queen of Spades*) There, you see! The Queen of Spades. An old woman will

bring bad luck! I don't know who this old boiler is, but I'm sure about the bad luck.

The doorbell rings

(*Consulting her watch*) Answer the door would you, Sophie? It's five to eight. It must be Monsieur D'Erignac.

Sophie goes out through Entrance 1

He always comes a little too early. (*She looks in a hand mirror and casually adjusts an errant lock of hair*)

Sophie enters

Sophie It's Monsieur D'Erignac, madame.
Césarine Show him in.
Sophie And another gentleman.
Césarine What!
Sophie A friend of his, madame. Would like to be introduced.
Césarine A stranger! And I look a wreck! Show them in, Sophie and then come and attend to me.

Sophie goes out Entrance 1

Césarine goes to Entrance 2 and opens the door. She is greeted by a torrent of barking

Niniche! Be quiet! Naughty dog!

Césarine goes in, shutting the door

The barking and her reprimands subside

Sophie shows in Fauvinard and Tardivaut who carries an extravagant bouquet of red roses. Both are in evening dress and slightly merry, Tardivaut tipsier than Fauvinard

Sophie This way, messieurs. Madame is at her toilet. If you would care to wait here, madame will not be long.
Fauvinard Excellent! Thank you, my girl. (*He hands her a coin, evidently a small one. She looks at it with disdain*)
Sophie Thank you, monsieur.

She goes off via Entrance 2

Fauvinard (*dropping into the armchair*) Make yourself at home. Park your bouquet.

Tardivaut (*putting the bouquet on the piano, throwing himself on to the chaise-longue*) Oof! My legs have given way. I think I've had too much champagne.

Fauvinard Me too.

Tardivaut (*looking round*) Nice place you've got here.

Fauvinard What's yours like up there?

Tardivaut Simpler, but very pleasant ... Look, are you sure you don't mind my waiting here until it's time for me to go up?

Fauvinard My dear fellow, what are friends for? I couldn't leave you out there on the street. The truth is, I still feel a little awkward and I could do with some support. I sometimes hear her voice, you see.

Tardivaut Whose?

Fauvinard My mother-in-law's. "Fauvinard! Fauvinard! What are you up to?" she's saying. She haunts me!

Tardivaut Ah, the voice of conscience!

Fauvinard No, just my mother-in-law.

Tardivaut Tell yourself she can't possibly be here.

Fauvinard I'll try. By the way, the only thing to watch out for here is Césarine's wretched little dog. (*Indicating the picture*) She bites.

Tardivaut I'll avoid her.

Césarine enters, even more glamorous than before

Both men rise, Tardivaut rather unsteadily

Césarine is followed by Sophie

Césarine Gentlemen, I do apologize for keeping you waiting.

Fauvinard Allow me, madame, to present to you a friend of mine, Monsieur de Tardenville.

Tardivaut What?

Fauvinard Secretary of State ... Ministry of the Interior ... Much decorated ... Poet in his spare time ...

Césarine I'm very pleased to meet you, especially as you're a friend of Monsieur D'Erignac.

Tardivaut D'Erignac?

Fauvinard That's me!

Tardivaut Now he tells me!

Césarine Please do sit down!

Fauvinard (*taking the bouquet from the top of the piano*) My dear
Césarine, will you do me the honour of accepting these few roses?

Tardivaut My roses!

Césarine Ah, Monsieur D'Erignac, you never forget how much I love
flowers. (*She smells them and puts them back on to the piano*)

Fauvinard They remind me of you, madame; and you never cease to
remind me about them!

Sophie goes via Entrance 4

Tardivaut Very well put! (*To Fauvinard*) Thief!

Fauvinard (*to Tardivaut*) You can take them back when you go
upstairs.

Césarine And how is the Ministry these days?

Tardivaut The Ministry?

Césarine Of the Interior.

Tardivaut Oh, the Ministry of the Interior! (*Beginning to feel rather
unwell*) Well, you know politics.

Fauvinard (*nodding sagely*) Politics ... Yes ...

Tardivaut (*swaying*) Sometimes we veer to the left.

Fauvinard (*holding him up*) Steady.

Tardivaut (*swaying*) Sometimes we veer to the right.

Fauvinard (*holding him up*) I knew you shouldn't have had that second
bottle of champagne.

Tardivaut And sometimes we ... Don't feel at all well. (*He nearly
collapses into Fauvinard's arms*)

Césarine Would you like some tea, Monsieur de Tardenville?

Tardivaut Eh? No, thank you, madame, I think I'll just have a little lie
down.

Césarine (*indicating Entrance 2*) Well, why not go in there for a while,
then.

Fauvinard Only for a little while. We might need that later on.

Tardivaut Thank you so much, madame. I feel quite ... Overwhelmed.

Tardivaut goes into Entrance 2

Césarine What a strange man!

Fauvinard He's a politician. He's under a lot of pressure ... From all
sides ...

*Sound of frenzied barking and a cry from Tardivaut who comes bounding
out clutching a bloodstained handkerchief to his right hand*

Tardivaut That damned poodle bit me!

Césarine Oh, she is a naughty girl! (*Opening the door to Entrance 2 and calling in*) Bad girl! Naughty Niniche!

A yap. She closes the door

Tardivaut I think I'd better go upstairs now.
Fauvinard (*explaining*) He has a friend upstairs.
Tardivaut She should have had her last music lesson by now.
Fauvinard Mademoiselle Zizi.
Césarine Oh, Zizi! Why didn't you say? Lovely girl. Very musical. You're not one of her music teachers, are you?
Tardivaut Not exactly.
Césarine I'll take you up there. I wanted a word with her about something.
Tardivaut So kind, madame. I'm still feeling a bit ——

Sophie enters with a vase of water. Tardivaut is just about to take the roses from the piano when Sophie removes them, puts them in the vase and puts the vase on a side table

My flowers!

Césarine escorts Tardivaut off via Entrance 1

Césarine (*as they go*) Did little Niniche nip you, then?
Tardivaut (*off*) It's bleeding rather badly. I do hope she's not rabid.

Their voices fade into the distance. Sophie continues to arrange flowers at the table. Fauvinard goes to the piano and plays the odd note on it

Fauvinard Sophie, I was wondering. (*Indicating Entrance 2*) I might be needing to use that room later on. There's an animal in there.
Sophie Niniche.
Fauvinard That's right. I wonder if you might like to move it somewhere else.
Sophie I don't know about that, monsieur.
Fauvinard (*producing a coin*) I'd be most grateful.
Sophie (*taking the money*) I'll see what I can do.

Sophie goes to Entrance 2. She opens the door and is met by a torrent of aggressive barks and growls. She manages to shut the door just in time

It's no good, monsieur. Niniche doesn't like me.
Fauvinard Does she like anyone?

Sophie I'll try my cousin Thérèse. She's from the country. She ought to be able to manage dogs.

Sophie goes off at Entrance 4

(*Off*) Thérèse!

Fauvinard (*idly picking out a tune — "Pierrot" — on the piano and half singing*) "Au clair de la lune, mon ami Pierrot ..."

Thérèse (*off, over the singing*) Where are you?

Sophie (*off*) Can you come here a moment?

Thérèse (*off*) This apartment is like a rabbit warren.

Fauvinard (*stopping playing*) I know that voice! (*He goes to look off Entrance 4*)

Sophie (*off*) Can you help me with something?

Thérèse (*off*) Anything I can do to —— ?

Fauvinard My God! It's Thérèse, my ex-cook. What's she doing here?

Fauvinard looks round for a place to escape to as the voices approach. He goes to Entrance 2, opens the door and looks in. Sound of yapping and growling. Fauvinard shuts the door quickly

Oh, God, no!

Sophie and Thérèse enter from Entrance 4

Sophie If you could move this little dog somewhere else. She needs a firm hand.

Over this Fauvinard, unable to decide on an exit, puts his collar up and crouches over the piano, bangs at the notes, plays scales very ineptly, etc.

Thérèse I don't know about that.

She sees Fauvinard who turns his head away from her and crouches lower over the piano

Who's this?

Fauvinard (*in a gruff voice, banging the keys*) Tuning the piano! Tuning the piano!

Thérèse (*coming towards him*) That's no way to tune a piano. My father was a piano tuner and ——

Sophie (*drawing her away from Fauvinard, towards Entrance 2*) Never mind about that now. I want you to handle this dog for me.
Thérèse Well, I don't know ...

Fauvinard continues to bang on the keys

That's a very odd man.
Sophie Thérèse, if you want to stay here tonight, you help me with this dog, understand? (*She pushes Thérèse through Entrance 2*)

Thérèse exits, Entrance 2

Sophie shuts the door

(*To Fauvinard*) Are you all right, monsieur?

Fauvinard has stopped playing and is turning down his collar

Fauvinard Never better. (*Reprising his song and piano accompaniment with a show of nonchalance*) "Au clair de la lune, mon ami Pierrot ..."
Sophie (*with a concerned look*) Very well, monsieur.

Sophie goes off at Entrance 4

Fauvinard immediately goes to the door of Entrance 2 and listens. The key is in the lock. A loud burst of growling and barking. Fauvinard locks the door and pockets the key

Thérèse (*off*) Aah! You little monster! (*She rattles at the door of Entrance 2*) Let me out! Let me out!

Further yapping and growling

Fauvinard I must go! Sophie!

Sophie comes out of Entrance 4

Sophie Yes, monsieur?
Fauvinard I have to go out for a little — fresh air — walk — I'll be back when Thérèse has finished with the dog.
Sophie How's she getting on with Niniche?
Fauvinard Very well, I think! Very well!

There's a further outburst of yapping and growling

Sophie (*not wanting to know*) Oh good!

Sophie goes off Entrance 4

A little confused, Fauvinard decides to go off via Entrance 3. He opens the door to see Thérèse standing in the doorway clutching a bloodstained handkerchief to her right hand

Thérèse This apartment is like a rabbit warren. Lucky there was another door to the bedroom — Oh!
Fauvinard Ah!
Thérèse Monsieur Fauvinard!
Fauvinard Yes. I was just passing. And ——
Thérèse Were you tuning the piano just now?
Fauvinard In a way. Yes.
Thérèse Sophie said Madame's lover was here.
Fauvinard Is he? Well, in that case, I'd better be on my way.
Thérèse It's you, isn't it, monsieur?

Slight pause

Fauvinard Look ... You won't go back and tell my wife or her mother, will you? (*Searching his pockets*) How about twenty francs?
Thérèse (*holding up her wounded hand*) I've been bitten.
Fauvinard So I see ... Forty?
Thérèse Thank you, monsieur. And I'll want a proper reference.
Fauvinard (*handing her some money*) Keep the change.

Césarine enters through Entrance 1. She has a rather showy ring on her hand

Thérèse (*looking at the money*) That's nothing like forty ——
Fauvinard (*seeing Césarine*) Yes, thank you! I'll write that — thing for you. (*He goes over to the desk and begins writing*) That will be all, Thérèse. For the moment.
Thérèse I'll be back for it.
Cesarine Thank you, Thérèse.

Thérèse goes off via Entrance 4

You're not looking for a cook are you, by any chance, Monsieur D'Erignac? (*Trying to see what he's writing*)

Fauvinard (*crumpling up the paper he is writing on*) Well, actually —
No! No, certainly not!
Césarine She's a good cook, as cooks go.
Fauvinard But I don't know her at all! (*He begins to write again*)
Césarine I never said you did! Now at last, we're alone together. (*She spreads herself on the chaise-longue and beckons him over*) Come and sit next to me.

Fauvinard crumples up his writing again and obeys

I've got something to show you.
Fauvinard Oh, good! I've been looking forward to this. (*Sitting close to her, undoing the ribbons on her negligée*) What is it?
Césarine (*thrusting out her hand with the ring on it*) What do you think?
Fauvinard Yes, very nice. (*To change the subject*) I didn't know you had a new servant.
Césarine The jeweller sent it to me on approval. Is it worth keeping on?
Fauvinard Well, it all depends.
Césarine On what?
Fauvinard On whether you like her cooking.
Césarine Whose?

Thérèse opens the door of Entrance 4

Thérèse Monsieur, my reference —— (*She is unseen and ignored so listens in*)
Fauvinard Thérèse. She's very good — so I'm told.
Thérèse I should think so too! That's the least he can say.
Césarine (*holding out the ring again, her back to Thérèse*) You know perfectly well what I'm talking about. I sent you the receipt.
Fauvinard Oh, that! I'd rather discuss Thérèse.
Césarine Well, what do you think?
Fauvinard (*examining the ring*) You want my opinion?
Thérèse Yes.
Césarine Why not?
Fauvinard All right then — worthless! Not genuine!
Thérèse How dare he!
Césarine Do you think so?
Fauvinard Yes, flashy and cheap-looking. Not worth the money. Return to where it came from.
Césarine All right, I will!

Thérèse The traitor! I'll have my revenge!

Thérèse goes

Cesarine There's a pair of pearl earrings I've got my eye on which you might like better. A bargain at four thousand.

Fauvinard Four thousand now! Yes, well, let's discuss that at some more convenient time. (*Undoing the ribbons on her negligée*) There are more pressing matters ——

Sophie enters from Entrance 1

Sophie Madame! Madame!

Césarine What is it?

Sophie It's — (*low in Césarine's ear*) Monsieur de Bagnolles!

Fauvinard (*aside*) De Bagnolles! The man I'm supposed to be divorcing!

Césarine Oh, what a nuisance! (*To Fauvinard*) I'm so sorry. An unexpected call. It's rather necessary that we are not seen together.

Fauvinard This always seems to happen to me, just as I'm getting started. (*Making towards Entrance 1*) My hat, Sophie.

Sophie Not that way, monsieur! He's coming up the stairs. He'll be at the front door any minute.

Césarine (*indicating Entrance 2*) You can get out of the back way through here. (*Trying to open the door*) It's locked!

Fauvinard (*going to Entrance 4*) This way!

Césarine No. Wait! I've got a better idea. Sophie, go and tell him that him that I'm feeling ill. That I've got the doctor with me. (*Indicating Fauvinard*) This doctor.

Sophie Yes, madame.

Sophie goes

Fauvinard I'm not feeling too well myself.

Césarine No! You don't understand. You have to be the doctor.

Fauvinard Must I? What does this man de Bagnolles want with you? He's not your lover, is he?

Césarine Yes! No! Not exactly ... (*Improvising*) He wants to be! That's it! That's why he's such a nuisance. He's very passionate about me. (*Remembering*) Extremely ... (*Recollecting herself*) I mean, he might do anything ... And often does ... He can be violent ... Extremely ... We must get rid of him. That's why you have to be a doctor. Turn down the lamp!

Fauvinard takes the lamp off the piano and is about to put it on the floor

I said turn it down, not put it down.

Fauvinard returns the lamp to the piano and turns it down while she arranges herself in an attitude of sickness on the chaise longue

Bring that chair up!

Fauvinard takes a chair from the round table and brings it up to her side

Now take my pulse.

Fauvinard sits but dithers

My pulse!

Fauvinard takes her wrist but he trembles so much he shakes it violently

Good God, you're trembling like a leaf. Keep still!

Fauvinard holds one hand still with the other. Sophie puts her head round the door

Sophie Shh!
Césarine He's coming!

Sophie enters, closely followed by Monsieur de Bagnolles, a serious man in his 30s, passionately in love with Césarine

(*Speaking in a weak voice*) So you don't think it's too serious? (*Low, to Fauvinard*) Answer me!
Fauvinard Your corpuscles are somewhat dilated, madame, and I detect a lengthening of the cerebellum, but ——
Césarine (*low, to Fauvinard*) That's enough!
Sophie Madame, it's Monsieur!
Césarine (*to Bagnolles*) My dear friend, I wasn't expecting you this evening.
Bagnolles No. It was an impulse ... (*Restraining his passion in front of the "doctor"*) Madame. Are you unwell?

Fauvinard rises and begins to sidle towards Entrance 1

Césarine Very unwell ... And without the good doctor here ... Where is he?

Bagnolles (*bringing Fauvinard back to Césarine*) No! No! Don't go on my account! I don't want to chase you away! (*He sits Fauvinard next to Césarine again*)

Fauvinard By all means. Of course! Yes!

Cesarine You were about to give me a prescription, weren't you, doctor?

Fauvinard (*rising*) What? Yes.

Cesarine (*pointing*) Use the desk over there. There's pen and ink and paper in the drawer.

Fauvinard Yes. Of course! Good! (*He hurries over to the desk and gets out paper and starts scribbling on it messily and nervously with a dip pen during the ensuing*)

Bagnolles At the last moment someone gave me a box for the opera. And of course, I thought of you.

Cesarine Impossible, I'm afraid.

Bagnolles So I see!

Cesarine You'd better go by yourself.

Bagnolles (*with restrained passion*) No. No, I couldn't face it without you. I'll go home. (*Going over to Fauvinard*) Now then, doctor, what are you prescribing?

Fauvinard (*trying to hide the paper from Bagnolles*) Ah! Yes! Well ...

Bagnolles takes the paper from Fauvinard and scrutinizes it. It is a horrible muddle of blots and scribbles

Bagnolles I can't make out a word of this.

Fauvinard Well, no! Quite. I'm a doctor.

Bagnolles So what are you prescribing?

Fauvinard Well ... Um ... A purgative ...

Bagnolles Yes?

Fauvinard An emetic ... Um ... And a laxative!

Bagnolles What! All at once?

Fauvinard No! One after the other ... Later ... Tomorrow. If she doesn't get better.

Césarine Do thank the doctor for me. He's been so kind!

Bagnolles (*embracing Fauvinard very emotionally*) My dear doctor!

Fauvinard Don't mention it. Please!

Bagnolles Are you sure it's not serious?

Fauvinard No, no! Not too serious.

Bagnolles Oh, thank God!
Fauvinard Just a little fatigue ... Too much ... Overwork ... er ...
Bagnolles Overwork? What work?
Fauvinard Over ... Over a period a period of time it should clear up.
Bagnolles What should clear up?
Fauvinard Whatever it is ... The fatigue.
Bagnolles (*solemnly*) Doctor, I am relying on you.
Fauvinard Yes. You may rely on me.
Bagnolles I leave her in your hands.
Fauvinard Fear not, monsieur!

Fauvinard and Bagnolles shake hands

Bagnolles (*to Césarine*) Good-night, Césarine.
Césarine Good-night, my friend.

Bagnolles goes to the door, then turns back. A thought strikes him

Bagnolles This isn't your usual doctor, is it?
Césarine No, he isn't usual. He's different ... I had to change him ... The other one, I mean. He became too friendly.
Bagnolles I see. Well ... Get some sleep. (*To Fauvinard with a hand on his shoulder*) Put her to bed.
Fauvinard I shall.
Bagnolles (*to Césarine*) I'll see you in the morning. (*To Fauvinard*) Let me know if there are any developments.
Fauvinard I'll do that.
Bagnolles Good-night!
Césarine Good-night!
Bagnolles (*tipping Sophie*) This is for you. Look after her, won't you?
Sophie Yes, monsieur. Thank you, monsieur.

Bagnolles and Sophie go out via Entrance 1. The door closes

Fauvinard (*collapsing on to the chaise-longue next to her*) Ouf!
Césarine Shussh! He may not have gone yet! (*She goes to the door and looks out*)
Fauvinard I'm more dead than alive.

Sophie enters

Sophie He's gone.

Fauvinard Thank heaven for that. (*He takes out a handkerchief from his pocket to mop his brow and in doing so dislodges the key to Entrance 2 that he had pocketed*)

Césarine That's the key to my bedroom. What were you doing with that? Sophie, put it back.

Sophie picks up the key, replaces it in the lock of Entrance 2 and exits via Entrance 4

Are you all right?

Fauvinard Yes. Fine. All I want is to be alone with you. The trouble is, even when I am, I keep hearing her voice.

Césarine Whose? Your wife's?

Fauvinard No. My mother-in-law's.

Césarine Just tell yourself she can't possibly be here. (*She sits on the chaise-longue*) Come and sit down next to me.

Fauvinard (*sitting next to her, once more undoing the ribbons on her negligée*) Alone at last!

A noise from outside of someone rushing down stairs and along the passage. Fauvinard starts up

Oh, my God, what's that?

Césarine (*rising*) Who on earth —— ?

Tardivaut comes tumbling through Entrance 4 out of breath. His right hand has now been neatly bandaged, but there are still signs of blood on it

Tardivaut Oh, my dear chap!

Césarine Monsieur de Tardenville!

Tardivaut Eh? Who? What? Where?

Fauvinard What's going on?

Tardivaut Hide me! Hide me somewhere, I beg you!

Fauvinard Why?

Tardivaut It's the old man! The old man! He's just arrived! Zizi's protector. She just had time to put me in the kitchen when he came in. Then I came down the service staircase into your apartment. But I'm sure he saw me. I think he's coming down after me.

He goes to look out of Entrance 4. Fauvinard follows

He's followed me! He's coming! There he is!

Fauvinard (*looking out*) My God, it's Gatinet!

Fauvinard rushes round looking for somewhere to hide. Tardivaut follows

Fauvinard goes in to Entrance 2 and shuts the door

Tardivaut tries to get in too but Fauvinard is holding the door shut on the other side

Tardivaut (*banging on the door*) Let me in!

Gatinet enters breathless

Gatinet I do beg your pardon, madame, for bursting in on you in this unexpected manner. But I thought I saw an intruder in the kitchen upstairs. He was escaping by the service ... Um. So I came down the same way hoping to ... You haven't seen an intruder by any chance?
Césarine No. I don't think so.
Gatinet (*to Tardivaut who is making his way stealthily towards Entrance 3*) What about you, monsieur?
Tardivaut Who? Me?
Gatinet Have you seen an intruder?
Tardivaut No! Absolutely not! (*He starts to go through Entrance 3*)
Césarine Please don't go on my account, monsieur. We still have things to discuss.
Gatinet (*aside*) Charming couple!
Césarine (*to Gatinet*) So, as you can see there is no one but us here.

There is barking and growling from Entrance 2, then a cry of pain from Fauvinard

That's just Niniche! (*She backs towards Entrance 2*)
Gatinet Zizi?
Césarine No, Niniche, my little dog.

There is renewed barking. She opens the door and looks in

Be quiet, Niniche! You naughty little dog! (*She shuts the door*)
Gatinet Ah, I see. I was talking about the young lady upstairs. Zizi. A very well-educated girl.
Césarine Yes. Charming. We were discussing her only just now.
Gatinet (*to Tardivaut*) You know her then?

Tardivaut Not in the least!

Gatinet She gets so excited about seeing me, the dear little thing. In fact she was so excited when she saw me this evening she fainted. So I went into the kitchen to get some smelling salts and that's when I saw the intruder. About your height I think, monsieur, or perhaps a little taller.

Tardivaut Oh, much taller!

Gatinet You may be right, monsieur. And there was something wrong with his right hand too.

Tardivaut puts his bandaged right hand behind his back

I wonder if I could borrow some smelling salts.

While he rambles on Césarine goes to the desk drawer and gets out a bottle of smelling salts. Gatinet is following Tardivaut about. Tardivaut is trying to avoid him

I think she was particularly upset because I was so late. I tend to fall asleep, you see. During the day. At night I'm fine ... Generally speaking ... It's all very odd ...

Césarine (*holding up the bottle of smelling salts*) Smelling salts, did you say?

Gatinet Most kind of you, madame! (*Low to Tardivaut, nudging him*) Apologies for spoiling your little er ... tête-á-tête. (*He winks at him*)

Tardivaut Monsieur! I —— !

Gatinet (*low to Tardivaut, nudging him*) Say no more! I'm a widower myself. (*He winks at him*)

Sophie rushes on from Entrance 1

Sophie Madame! Madame! (*Low to Césarine*) It's Monsieur de Bagnolles! He's come back!

Césarine Drat!

Sophie He'll be here any minute.

Gatinet Eh? Who? (*He reaches out for the smelling salts*)

Césarine (*snatching them away*) Stay a moment, monsieur.

Bagnolles enters, Entrance 1

Bagnolles Terrible news! I had to come back and —— (*He sees the others*) Oh! I do beg your pardon, gentlemen ...

Césarine Ah, yes! These people were just borrowing some smelling salts off me for the girl on the second floor who's fainted.

Gatinet Ah, yes, Thank you! Well I shall leave you two gentlemen to your er — So sorry to have disturbed you both.
Césarine Drat!
Bagnolles (*indicating Tardivaut*) So this gentleman is ——?
Césarine Ah, this ——! Yes. He's the — the doctor!
Bagnolles Another doctor?
Césarine That's right. He was called in. Second opinion.
Bagnolles He isn't your usual doctor either, is he?
Césarine No. Very unusual. You see, he's ... A homeopath.
Gatinet Ah, monsieur, I didn't know you were a doctor.
Tardivaut I'm a homeopath.
Césarine Doctor Tardenville.
Gatinet I wonder, doctor, if you would come and see my Zizi who's just fainted. I'm sure she'd appreciate it.
Tardivaut If you really think I could help ...?
Gatinet You could prescribe a tincture.
Tardivaut I could give her one. Yes.
Gatinet If madame can spare him ...?
Césarine Please feel free. (*She hands Tardivaut the smelling salts*) The smelling salts, doctor.
Gatinet I'll bring them back as soon as we've finished with them. And the doctor too!
Césarine Oh, please! Take your time!
Gatinet This way, doctor.
Tardivaut Thank you, monsieur. I think I know the way.

They go off via Entrance 1

Césarine moves to Entrance 2 and listens at the door

Bagnolles How are you feeling now?
Césarine What? Oh! A little better.
Bagnolles You seem very nervous.

He moves towards her. She moves towards him to prevent him coming nearer to Entrance 2

Césarine So what's happened?
Bagnolles Oh, my dear, Madame de Bagnolles knows all!
Césarine Hell!
Bagnolles I'd just got home when the maid who happens to be in my confidence told me everything. My wife has informed the police. She wants to catch us *in flagrante*!

Césarine Tonight?

Bagnolles She went to see a lawyer this very afternoon, Counsellor Fauvinard. He recommended drastic action. I shall be ruined. I will lose all her money! You must understand. At all costs a scandal should be avoided. For all our sakes. (*Choking with emotion*) And so ... This has to be ... Goodbye!

Césarine (*playing up to him*) You're leaving me!

Bagnolles I must! Tomorrow morning I pay a call on this Counsellor Fauvinard and see if I can't do something to prevent this frightful business. Then I think I shall go away for a while. Italy perhaps. To try to forget ... Everything. Perhaps on my return my wife may think differently. (*Taking her hands, with deep emotion*) Oh, my dear, we must be strong!

The sound of yapping and growling from Entrance 2

Césarine Oh, my God! (*She rushes to the Entrance 2, opens the door and hisses in*) Will you keep her quiet! (*She shuts the door*)

Bagnolles What did you say?

Césarine (*opening the door*) Be quiet, you naughty, naughty dog! (*She shuts the door*)

Bagnolles What on earth's going on?

Césarine It's Niniche. She's not been the same since — something happened to her.

Further yapping

Bagnolles This is intolerable. Let me deal with this.

Césarine (*barring his way*) No. No, you can't!

Further yapping

Bagnolles Why not? She needs a firm hand.

Césarine She hates men. So would you if one of them had sat on you while you were in my muff. (*Dragging him over to the chaise-longue*) Don't interfere with the dog! Please, leave me. This is all too much! (*Collapsing back on to the chaise longue*) My nerves! My nerves!

Further yapping

Aah! This is a nightmare!

Bagnolles I can't leave you like this. (*He bends over her on the chaise longue, an apparently compromising position*)

Gatinet enters with smelling salts, Entrance 4

Gatinet Oh! Ah! Sorry to disturb your little er ... *tête-á-tête.* Just returning the smelling salts.
Bagnolles Give them to me. (*He grabs the smelling salts from Gatinet and thrusts them under Césarine's nose*)
Césarine Aaah!

The dog starts yapping and growling again

Aaah! (*Very loud and hysterical*) Oh! Kill it! Just kill it! It's driving me mad! Mad! Aah!
Gatinet Kill who?

A single yap, then the sound of a dog being throttled

Césarine (*regaining control*) Nothing! Nobody!
Bagnolles (*tending to her*) Just an attack of nerves.
Gatinet Ah, yes! It's exactly the same upstairs.
Bagnolles What!
Gatinet Funny thing, nerves. I went up there, you know with your friend Doctor ... The homeopath. The girl Zizi was up and seemed fine, and then, dammit, as soon as she sees the doctor, she shouts out "Oh my God, not you!" And faints all over again.

Gatinet sits on a chair and his speech gets more slurred. The other two watch him as he drifts off into oblivion

Very odd ... I said to him ... The homeopath fellow ... I said, "Do you know her, because she said 'Oh My God, not you!' or something." He said: "Know her? I don't know her from a hole in the ..." What's his name ... (*His head drops. He snores*)
Césarine He's unconscious. You must go now. Quickly.
Bagnolles But I can't leave you alone like this!
Césarine Oh, I won't be — I mean, I need a little time to take it all in — your leaving me so suddenly.
Bagnolles (*passionately kneeling before her*) How could I ever leave you?

Gatinet snores

Césarine Oh, but you must! I mean — for the sake of your money — your marriage — your honour!

Bagnolles You think of everything!
Césarine You will write to me, won't you?
Bagnolles Every day!
Césarine As often as you can will do.
Bagnolles (*embracing her*) You must be very brave, my sweet!
Césarine I shall think of you always.

Bagnolles and Césarine kiss. Gatinet snores

Bagnolles (*breaking off*) Oh, this is ridiculous! (*He goes over and shakes Gatinet*) Hey! You! Wake up!
Gatinet (*half conscious*) Oh my God, not you! Eh? What? Who? I do beg your pardon. You see. It's a funny thing, but whenever I sit down I start to fall ... (*Beginning to nod again*) Start to fall ...
Bagnolles (*shaking him and dragging him to his feet*) Wake up! Wake up! You can't sleep here with this lady!
Césarine Well, goodbye, gentlemen.
Gatinet Yes, I think I shall take a turn in the street. Get some fresh air. That should do the trick.
Césarine And what about Mademoiselle Zizi?
Gatinet Oh, she's fine! She's got the doctor up there giving her a thorough going over. (*To Bagnolles*) You coming?
Bagnolles My darling Césarine, I will write every ——
Césarine Yes, I know! Every day! Go! Go!
Gatinet Madame, it has been a pleasure.

Gatinet and Bagnolles go towards Entrance 1

(*To Bagnolles, as they go*) Yes, you see, at night I'm generally fine. I'm a bit of a night bird ... Night ... Hedgehog? No. Night ... whatyoumecallit ... Sort of thing ...

Gatinet and Bagnolles exit

As Gatinet's voice drones into the distance Césarine goes to Entrance 2

(*Off*) Owl! That's the fellow! On the other hand if I have to sit down, I can suddenly find myself dropping off to er ... If you know what I mean ...
Césarine (*knocking on the bedroom door*) You can come out now.

Fauvinard enters, pale, dishevelled, tie askew, clothes slightly torn. His right hand is crudely bandaged with a handkerchief, blood seeping through. Under his left arm he carries the corpse of Niniche, the poodle

Fauvinard All clear?
Césarine Look at the state of you! What have you got there?
Fauvinard (*holding up the dead dog*) It's Niniche. I had to ...
Césarine Dead?
Fauvinard It was the only way to silence it.
Césarine Yes, but — dead! You've killed her.
Fauvinard You told me to. I'll have it stuffed if you like.
Césarine Was she biting a lot?
Fauvinard I won't say her bark was worse than her bite. They were as bad as each other. You don't think she might have been rabid, do you?
Césarine Rabid? I expect she was furious!
Fauvinard I mean do you think she had rabies?
Césarine Don't be ridiculous! We haven't got rabies here. (*Undoing his handkerchief and examining the cut*) I will admit it is rather a nasty nip. I think I'll ... (*distracted by the dead dog under his left arm*) Oh, do get rid of that thing somewhere. It's putting me off.

Fauvinard puts it on the piano

No! Not on the piano!

Fauvinard picks it up and puts it on the table

And not on the table. Do have some common sense!

Fauvinard picks it up and Césarine takes it from him

(*Not knowing what to do with it*) Oh! (*She puts it under the table so it is mostly hidden by the cloth, but the head sticks out*) Well, it can go there for the time being. I'll see about it later. Now I'd better go and find a proper bandage for that bite.
Fauvinard Must you leave me? Alone in a room, with a dead dog.
Césarine Oh, don't be such a baby! (*She goes to leave via Entrance 4*)

The doorbell rings

Answer that, will you, Sophie?

Césarine exits

Sophie (*off*) Yes, madame!

Fauvinard (*seeing the dog's head poking out from under the tablecloth*) Ah!

He takes it out from under the table thinking to put it somewhere else. Then he stops as he hears voices

Sophie (*off*) Good-evening, madame! Can I help you?

Laiguisier (*off*) I wish to speak to your mistress.

Fauvinard Aah! I must be going mad! I keep hearing her voice in my head. Just tell yourself she can't possibly be here.

Sophie (*off*) I'm sorry, madame, but Madame is indisposed.

Laiguisier (*off*) Never mind that! I wish to speak to your mistress.

Fauvinard She's saying she wants to speak to my mistress. I'm crazy. (*He puts his hands up to his head holding the dog*) Aah! (*He puts them down*)

Sophie (*off*) You can't come in here, madame.

Fauvinard (*going to Entrance 1*) What is going on? (*Looking*) My God! It really is her!

In a panic he desperately looks round for somewhere to hide. Having no time to exit he dives under the table still holding the dead dog just as Laiguisier is entering the room

Laiguisier (*off*) Don't be impertinent, girl! Let me pass!

Laiguisier enters followed by Sophie. She carries an umbrella

Now, will you please go and fetch your mistress.

Sophie Very good, madame.

Sophie goes off via Entrance 4. Laiguisier inspects the furnishings critically. She sees a movement in the tablecloth

Laiguisier Who is that under there? What are you doing? (*She tentatively begins to lift the tablecloth*)

Fauvinard begins to bark and growl

Oh, a dog. Come along doggie! Nice dog. (*She tentatively puts her hand under the tablecloth*)

Fauvinard barks and growls

Aah! (*She withdraws her hand. She has been bitten*) Aah!

The head of the dead dog emerges from under the tablecloth and wags about

Naughty dog! (*She hits it with her umbrella*)

A yap. The head withdraws

Césarine enters

Césarine Excuse me, madame?
Laiguisier Ah, there you are! Your dog has just bitten me.
Césarine That's impossible.

Fauvinard throws the dead dog from under the table

Laiguisier (*holding up her hand*) Look at this!
Césarine My dog can't have bitten you. It's dead. (*She looks for it under the table and sees Fauvinard, then sees the dog*)
Laiguisier Don't be ridiculous!
Césarine (*picking up the dead dog*) That is a dead dog.
Laiguisier Well, it wasn't dead when it bit me.
Césarine (*placing it on the table*) So why is it dead now?
Laiguisier Madame! I have not come here to discuss dead dogs. I have come here about the Veauradieux Case.
Césarine (*alarmed*) What do you know about that?
Laiguisier My son-in-law is a lawyer, and he ——
Césarine It has nothing to do with me. Now will you please leave ——
Laiguisier Certainly not.

The doorbell rings

Césarine Well, I haven't time to discuss it now. That's the doorbell. (*She pushes her into Entrance 2*) Will you go and wait in there for the moment.
Laiguisier (*being reluctantly propelled through the door*) I merely want to ask you a few simple questions about these receipts for jewellery.

Laiguisier exits Entrance 2

Cesarine Later. (*She shuts the door on her, locks it and pockets the key. To Fauvinard under the table*) You can come out now.

Fauvinard half emerges

Sophie enters from Entrance 1

What is it, Sophie?
Sophie It's that man again. Monsieur Gatinet.

Fauvinard retreats under the table again

He says it's urgent.
Césarine Show him in.

Sophie goes

(*Looking under the table*) What are you doing under there? You can come out now!

Fauvinard begins to emerge again

Sophie enters

Sophie Monsieur Gatinet!
Fauvinard Aah! (*He retreats under the table again*)

Gatinet enters

Gatinet Ah, madame! You have been so gracious, I felt I had to warn you. I was in the street taking some fresh air and ——
Césarine Sophie! (*Indicating Entrance 2*) There's a woman in there I don't want to get out. Will you lock the other entrance to the bedroom?
Sophie Yes, madame!

Sophie goes out via Entrance 3 to do this

Césarine Now, monsieur?
Gatinet Yes, well, I was in the street taking some fresh air. I have this habit of falling asleep ——
Césarine Yes, yes! Go on!

Sophie enters from Entrance 3

Gatinet And I saw a carriage arrive. It was the police. The Commissioner and some officers. I overheard their conversation. They're going to raid this apartment.

Césarine Thank you, monsieur! Sophie, I must change. You will answer the door. When I next appear, it will not be as your mistress. Do you understand?

Sophie Yes, madame!

Gatinet Eh?

Césarine And you will confirm that, won't you? Monsieur, I am eternally in your debt.

Césarine goes out via Entrance 4

Gatinet Eh?

Sophie All right, monsieur?

Sophie hurries out after Césarine

Gatinet looks nervously round the room. He sees the dead dog on the table and starts nervously. Laiguisier angrily rattles the door of Entrance 2. Gatinet starts again

Gatinet Aah!

Laiguisier (*off*) What is going on? Let me out of here!

Gatinet I know that voice! (*He goes to the door and tries it. It is locked*)

Laiguisier rattles the handle from the other side

Laiguisier (*off*) Who's that? Let me out!

Gatinet Ah! It's her.

Gatinet bounds back from the door in time to see Fauvinard, his head covered with the tablecloth emerging from under the table. The dead dog falls to the floor

Aah!

Fauvinard blunders about, his head still covered to conceal his identity

The Commissioner bangs on the front door and rings the bell

Ah!

Commissioner (*off*) Open in the name of the law!

Gatinet Aah! The police!

Fauvinard takes a furtive glance from under his tablecloth and makes for Entrance 3

Commissioner enters with Sophie

Commissioner (*seeing Fauvinard at Entrance 3*) Stay where you are, monsieur. I am a Commissioner of Police.

Fauvinard freezes

(*To Sophie*) Will you fetch your mistress immediately.
Sophie She's not in, monsieur.
Commissioner Don't lie to me, mademoiselle! I am a Commissioner of Police. Go and fetch her at once.

Sophie goes off via Entrance 4

(*To officers off*) Stay there, officer. I want no one to escape from this apartment! (*To Gatinet*) And who are you, monsieur?
Gatinet Ah, well, I'm not here ... I was upstairs but I came down to ...
Commissioner Sit down, monsieur.
Gatinet (*retreating before him*) No, I wouldn't ask me to do that. You see when I sit down, I er ...
Commissioner (*very forcefully*) Sit down, monsieur!

Gatinet sits

Now then, monsieur ——

Gatinet nods off

Monsieur? Oh, really! (*Seeing Fauvinard trying to escape via Entrance 3*) Stop there, monsieur! No one escapes! Remove that cloth from your head!

Fauvinard lets it fall to the ground

Come here, monsieur!

Fauvinard obeys

Will you tell me who the gentleman asleep over there is?
Fauvinard Oh, nobody. He's just my uncle.
Commissioner I see. Now then, monsieur, what is your name?
Fauvinard Er ... D'Erignac.
Commissioner You would be well advised not to lie to a Commissioner of Police, monsieur. It can have very serious consequences.

Fauvinard (*despairingly*) Oh, very well! My name is Fauvinard.
Commissioner Oh, dear! Oh, dear! You're lying again aren't you, monsieur?
Fauvinard What?
Commissioner I thought I had made myself clear. Your name is not D'Erignac or Fauvinard. You are Monsieur de Bagnolles, aren't you, monsieur?
Fauvinard What? Oh. Yes! De Bagnolles. I admit it freely. I am Monsieur de Bagnolles.
Commissioner That's better! It so happens that Madame de Bagnolles saw you enter the building not long ago.
Fauvinard Yes, I am Monsieur de Bagnolles.
Commissioner Very well, monsieur, but I must ask you to accompany me to my office to sign certain documents.
Fauvinard Oh. Must I? Can't I do it here?
Commissioner I'm afraid not, monsieur. You will need to be formally identified by Madame de Bagnolles.
Fauvinard Oh, my God! My client!
Commissioner I beg your pardon, monsieur?
Fauvinard Nothing.
Commissioner Now I wish to speak to the lady with whom you have been committing the adultery. (*Calling off*) Mademoiselle?
Fauvinard I admit everything. Isn't that enough?
Commissioner All in good time, monsieur.

Thérèse enters from Entrance 4

Fauvinard Thérèse!
Commissioner And who are you, madame? Are you this man's lover?
Thérèse Certainly not, monsieur! I am the cook.
Commissioner Very well, madame. I am a Commissioner of Police and I wish to speak with your mistress. I will speak with her alone in here, so, monsieur, if you could step into that room for a moment. (*Indicating Entrance 3*)

Fauvinard starts to go

One moment, monsieur. To prevent your absconding, you will remove your coat and trousers.
Fauvinard This is an outrage!
Commissioner Do you wish me to ask an officer to help you with the task?
Fauvinard No! No!

Commissioner Then you will oblige me by obeying me.

Fauvinard removes these garments

You, madame, will take charge of Monsieur de Bagnolle's garments.
Fauvinard Oh, God!
Thérèse Monsieur de Bagnolles! He's not Monsieur de Bagnolles!
Commissioner Your loyalty is very commendable, madame, but quite useless. This man has already admitted that he is Monsieur de Bagnolles.
Fauvinard I've admitted it.
Thérèse Very good, monsieur.
Commissioner Give her the clothes, monsieur.

Fauvinard hands over the coat and trousers to Thérèse

I give you these as a sacred trust, madame. If you mislay them I shall hold you personally responsible.
Thérèse Very good, monsieur. Thank you, monsieur.

Thérèse goes off via Entrance 4 gleefully

Commissioner Now then, monsieur (*indicating Entrance 3*) I will trouble you to step in there for a few moments. I wish to interview the others in this case. But do not try to escape, monsieur! No one escapes! My officers are outside and you have no trousers.
Fauvinard When do I get my trousers back?
Commissioner A few formalities first, monsieur, and then your garments will be restored to you.

Fauvinard goes off via Entrance 3

(*Calling*) Mademoiselle?

Sophie appears from Entrance 1 followed by Césarine, now very soberly dressed

Sophie Yes, monsieur?
Césarine What is going on here?
Commissioner I am looking for the lady of this apartment who passes under the name of Césarine Chamotel but whose married name is Césarine Veauradieux. Are you she?
Césarine No. I'm Zizi from upstairs, aren't I, Sophie?

Sophie Yes, mademoiselle.
Césarine This is Sophie, her maid.
Commissioner I am aware of that, mademoiselle. (*To Sophie*) And where is your mistress?
Césarine (*nudging Sophie and pointing to Entrance 2*) In there.
Sophie (*pointing to Entrance 2*) In there.

Commissioner goes to the door. He finds it locked

Commissioner Why is this door locked?
Césarine She locked herself in. She was afraid. (*She passes the key to Sophie to whom she says sotto voce*) But you have a spare key!
Sophie But I have a spare key! (*She hands it to the Commissioner*)

Commissioner goes to open the door

Césarine I think I'll just slip back upstairs now.

Césarine goes out via Entrance 1

Commissioner Come out, madame!

Laiguisier emerges

Laiguisier What is the meaning of this? This is an outrage!
Commissioner I am a Commissioner of Police, madame.
Laiguisier Then explain to me what has been going on!
Commissioner All in good time, madame, but first if you would be so good as to tell us your name.
Laiguisier I am Madame Laiguisier.
Commissioner Oh, no it isn't, madame. It is Madame Veauradieux and I am arresting you not only for an adulterous act with Monsieur de Bagnolles but also for questioning in connection with the jewel robberies in the Rue Saint-Honoré.
Laiguisier What! This is an outrage! I have nothing to do with this.
Commissioner Oh, no! Madame, I have been long enough in my profession to know when someone is lying. Empty the contents of your bag.

Laiguisier does so on to the table

Aha! (*He picks out a crumpled piece of paper*) Then what is this? (*He reads it*) A receipt for jewellery with this address on it. Doubtless a forgery. So that's your game, madame! (*Calling off*) Officer, take this woman down to the carriage.

Laiguisier Wait a moment, Commissioner. This is absurd.

Gatinet snores

(*Seeing Gatinet asleep in the chair*) Good heavens! What is that man doing here?

Commissioner That, madame, as if you didn't know, is your lover's uncle.

Laiguisier My lover's uncle! Don't be ridiculous! That is my son-in-law's uncle.

Commissioner So! You are your son-in-law's lover, are you? You would add incest to your other crimes, would you?

Laiguisier Of course not! Don't be an imbecile!

Commissioner You call me, an officer of the law an imbecile, madame? You would add insult to incest! (*Calling off*) Officer, take this woman down to the carriage.

Laiguisier turns to go to Entrance 1

(*Seeing the dead dog*) One moment, madame! (*He picks up the dead dog*) May I ask what this is?

Laiguisier That is a dead dog.

Commissioner I am aware of that, madame. And what is a dead dog doing in your apartment?

Laiguisier How many times do I have to tell you, this is not my apartment! This dog bit me.

Commissioner It bit you?

Laiguisier Yes.

Commissioner And then it died?

Laiguisier Yes! It must have done.

Commissioner (*dropping the dog*) This is serious indeed, madame. I shall have to put you into quarantine immediately.

Laiguisier What!

Commissioner Go down at once to the carriage with the officer, madame. I shall follow shortly.

Laiguisier This is an outrage!

Commissioner Go this instant, madame!

Laiguisier obeys and exits

(*To Sophie*) Now where is the cook with Monsieur de Bagnolle's clothes?

Sophie (*calling off, Entrance 4*) Thérèse!

Thérèse appears almost immediately

Thérèse Yes, monsieur?
Commissioner I have a very serious case of suspected rabies on my hands. You are not to move from here until I return, do you understand? And you madame, you are not to give Monsieur de Bagnolles his coat and trousers.
Thérèse Certainly not, monsieur.
Commissioner Now then. Monsieur de Bagnolles? Where is Monsieur de Bagnolles?

Fauvinard emerges from Entrance 3

I shall have to deal with you later. Now I must take my leave of you.

Commissioner picks up the dead dog gingerly and goes off with it, followed by Sophie

Fauvinard Thérèse! He's gone! You can give me my trousers now.
Thérèse Certainly not, monsieur.
Fauvinard Thérèse! You were always a wonderful cook.
Thérèse A pity you never stood up for me then, isn't it, monsieur?
Fauvinard I must get away this minute! Wait a moment!

Fauvinard picks up the tablecloth and dashes into Entrance 2

Gatinet (*waking up and rising from his chair*) What's happening? Who are you?
Thérèse Monsieur Gatinet!
Gatinet No you're not. I'm Monsieur Gatinet. Do you take me for an imbecile?

Thérèse goes out with the coat and trousers. Fauvinard emerges, the tablecloth made into a makeshift dress, wearing a shawl and a hat with a veil, covering as much of his face as possible

Gatinet wakes again and sees him

Ah, good-evening, madame! You're a fine figure of a woman!

Gatinet pursues Fauvinard, trying to prevent him from leaving

Fauvinard Oh, go back to sleep!

Fauvinard pushes him on to the sofa and dashes out of Entrance 1

Gatinet falls asleep again

Thérèse enters again with some brown paper and the coat and trousers which she lays on the table and starts to wrap in the brown paper

Thérèse (*holding up Fauvinard's coat and trousers in the brown paper parcel in triumph*) Revenge!

Quickish fade

END OF ACT II

ACT III

Fauvinard's study, the following morning

Fanchette knocks, enters Entrance 1 and looks around

Fanchette Monsieur? Oh. That's funny.

Fauvinard looks round the door of Entrance 1

(*Seeing him*) Monsieur! You are up!
Fauvinard (*off*) What? Oh. Yes. I'm up.

Fauvinard enters the room. He is wearing a rather odd selection of clothes which don't really fit him. He looks very much the worse for wear, his hand is still bandaged and he has shaved off his whiskers. He carries a bundle under his arm which includes the tablecloth

Has madame left her room?
Fanchette Not yet, monsieur.
Fauvinard Thank goodness! Er ... Thank you.
Fanchette Monsieur is up and ... dressed very early.
Fauvinard I have been. I am.
Fanchette Monsieur has shaved off his whiskers.
Fauvinard Oh ... Yes. It's changed my appearance quite a lot, don't you think?
Fanchette Yes, monsieur, it's made you look a great deal uglier.
Fauvinard Ah ... Thank you. So you think people won't be able to recognize me?
Fanchette Well, monsieur, I would say that those who knew you would still be able to recognize you, but possibly not those who didn't.
Fauvinard Imbecile!
Fanchette It's a pity though. I liked monsieur's whiskers.

The doorbell rings

Fauvinard Next time I shave I shall make sure to consult you first. Answer that!
Fanchette Yes, monsieur.

*Fanchette exits. Fauvinard follows her to see who it is. Satisfied it is no
one dangerous, he returns and scrutinizes his face in a hand mirror*

Tardivaut enters with Fanchette

Monsieur Tardivaut.
Fauvinard Yes. Thank you. Leave us!

Fanchette goes

Tardivaut My dear fellow, I came to ask you what on earth's been
going on.
Fauvinard Oh, my dear friend!

They shake hands with their bandaged hands and both react in agony

Fauvinard }
Tardivaut } *(together)* Aaah!
Tardivaut Zizi said something about a Commissioner of Police.
Fauvinard Not only that. My mother-in-law.
Tardivaut Your mother-in-law!
Fauvinard It's a long story. Which reminds me, if you happen to meet
my mother-in-law you've got paralysis of the tongue.
Tardivaut Eh? Paralysis of the tongue? What d'you mean?
Fauvinard I mean you can't talk. You can make a noise if you like, but
you can't talk.
Tardivaut But why?
Fauvinard It's a long story. Too long. Will you do this for me?
Tardivaut All right. If I meet your mother-in-law I can make a noise,
but I can't talk.
Fauvinard It often affects me the same way.
Tardivaut What happened?
Fauvinard Well, you see. There we were, about to get started — Césarine
and me — when there was a knock, and it was the Commissioner. And
he'd been sent by Madame de Bagnolles and she told him to because
I'd told her to tell him.
Tardivaut I'm not following this.
Fauvinard It will all become perfectly clear. Don't interrupt. Well,
the Commissioner found me under a tablecloth and took away my
trousers. But I managed to get away and fortunately he thought I was
de Bagnolles.
Tardivaut Who's he?
Fauvinard He's the lover.

Tardivaut Whose lover?

Fauvinard My mistress's lover, but he's also the husband.

Tardivaut Whose husband?

Fauvinard My client's husband.

Tardivaut You were mistaken by the Commissioner of Police for your client's husband who is also your mistress's lover?

Fauvinard That's it in a nutshell. It's all quite simple. Anyway, I got away disguised in a hat and this tablecloth, as a sort of woman, and then I got a change of clothes off a man who also thought I was a sort of woman. We won't go into that. Then I went to a barber and got him to shave off my whiskers.

Tardivaut Yes, I was going to ask you ——

Fauvinard That's the clever part, you see, because it was dark at the time and with any luck the Commissioner won't recognize me without them.

Tardivaut As what?

Fauvinard As my mistress's lover which of course I was, but also as my client's husband, de Bagnolles, which I'm not.

Tardivaut I see. Do you think you ought to carry on with this case?

Fauvinard Well, I've got to, haven't I? Because she's coming to see me this morning.

Tardivaut Who?

Fauvinard Madame de Bagnolles.

Tardivaut Ah ... Does it still hurt?

Fauvinard What?

Tardivaut (*holding up his bandaged right hand*) This.

Fauvinard (*holding up his bandaged right hand*) Oh, that! Yes. Well, at least that problem's solved. Niniche is dead.

Tardivaut Ah ... Natural causes, I hope?

Fauvinard Perfectly natural. I strangled her.

Angèle and Fanchette are heard talking off

Shh! My wife! Not a word about this.

Tardivaut Not a word!

Angèle enters

Angèle I'm so sorry. Am I disturbing?

Fauvinard Not at all. (*Embracing her*) Good-morning, my dear. I'm up early as you see, busy as usual. You know my colleague Tardivaut? He wrote to me yesterday, you know.

Angèle Monsieur.

Tardivaut Charmed, madame.

Angèle And how is the Veauradieux case going?

Fauvinard What? Oh, well. Progress is being made, isn't it, Tardivaut?

Tardivaut Yes. Yes. We may need to consult further.

Fauvinard I'm not sure about that.

Angèle Armand! What's happened to your whiskers?

Fauvinard You noticed. Well, you know, I felt they were getting in the way.

Angèle Getting in the way of what? I liked them. You don't look nearly so handsome now.

Fauvinard Oh, good! I mean — do I really look different?

Angèle Yes, and those clothes ... Where did you get them? And what have you done to your hand?

Fauvinard Ah, yes, you see I cut myself shaving. When I was shaving my whiskers, you see.

Angèle (*noticing Tardivaut's hand*) Did you have a similar accident, monsieur?

Noises off. Laiguisier's voice can be heard

Tardivaut No, no. I have a different story altogether.

Fanchette enters at a run

Fanchette Monsieur! Madame's mother has just arrived.

Fauvinard Oh, my God!

Angèle I'll go and see to her.

Fanchette No, madame! It's Monsieur she wants to speak to.

Tardivaut I must be on my way.

Fauvinard (*clutching on to him*) No! No! For God's sake, stay with me!

He guides Tardivaut off through Entrance 3

Tardivaut exits

Wait for me in there.

Laiguisier enters Entrance 1 in a towering rage, carrying Fauvinard's coat and trousers in the brown paper parcel

Laiguisier Where is he? Where is he? Ah! There you are!

Angèle Good-morning, Mother.

Laiguisier Never mind that! (*To Fauvinard*) Where were you last night?

Fauvinard Well, I was ——

Laiguisier You're lying to me! Don't lie to me!

Fauvinard But ——

Laiguisier Don't lie to me! I have had the most dreadful night. I won't go into it in detail. I have been accused of adultery, jewel theft, of harbouring an unmentionable disease. I have been bitten, I have been medically examined in the most intimate and improper way, and when I finally get home, I find that these have been sent to me. (*She dumps them on Fauvinard's desk*) Together with an anonymous note.

Fauvinard I don't understand. What exactly ——?

Laiguisier You're lying to me! Don't lie to me! I presume that you are not going to tell me that you are wearing the clothes you wore last night.

Fauvinard No ... Not exactly.

Laiguisier So where are they?

Fauvinard Where are what?

Laiguisier Don't lie to me! I'll tell you where they are. They're here! (*She holds up the coat and trousers*) There! Fauvinard on the label. Do you deny that they are yours?

Angèle Oh, Armand! Did you have them stolen?

Fauvinard Well ——

Laiguisier Don't lie to me! This note came with them.

Fauvinard Are you going to believe an anonymous note?

Laiguisier (*reading*) It says: "Your son-in-law has been dabbling in the flesh pots." What a vulgar expression!

Fauvinard My God! Thérèse!

Laiguisier Don't lie to me! It says: "These garments were found by me in the first floor of an apartment in Eleven Rue Saint-Lazare."

Angèle Mother, what does it mean?

Laiguisier "Signed OLD BOILER". Impudence! Eleven Rue Saint-Lazare. I was there last night myself.

Fauvinard What on earth were you doing there?

Laiguisier Never mind that now. I want an explanation, and don't lie to me!

Fauvinard I don't deny that these are my clothes. Thank you very much for returning them to me, madame.

Laiguisier Get on with it, and don't lie to me!

Fauvinard Well, it's all a little difficult ——

Laiguisier I'm sure!

Fauvinard Because it involves my friend Tardivaut.

Laiguisier Don't lie to me!

Fauvinard You see ... I lent my clothes to him.
Laiguisier Don't lie to me!
Fauvinard He can corroborate.
Laiguisier How can he?
Fauvinard (*opening the door of Entrance 3*) Because he is here.
Tardivaut!

Tardivaut comes out

Laiguisier I meant how can he corroborate? He's got a paralysed
tongue.
Angèle What!
Fauvinard (*to Tardivaut*) You've got a paralysed tongue.

Tardivaut nods to Laiguisier

He can nod and make a noise but he can't talk very well.
Angèle I don't understand.
Laiguisier Very well then. Monsieur Tardivaut, can you — somehow
— explain why Monsieur Fauvinard gave you his trousers and how
you managed to lose them. And don't lie to me!
Fauvinard (*to Tardivaut*) Go on then! Make a noise or something.
Tardivaut (*with gestures*) Uuurgh ... Aaarggh ... Ooooh. Wuff! Wuff!
(*Etc.*)

*Tardivaut executes an elaborate pantomime with noises, suggestive of
drinking too much, being bitten by a dog, having the dog pee on him,
going for a swim, having his trousers stolen, borrowing Fauvinard's
etc. Ad lib, but not too long. The two women look on with increasing
scepticism and amazement*

Fauvinard Yes, well what he's saying is that unfortunately he ——
Angèle Wait! I don't understand. Monsieur Tardivaut was talking
perfectly to me just now. What's the matter?
Laiguisier Are you deceiving me, Monsieur Tardivaut?
Tardivaut Er ...
Laiguisier This is an outrage. You're lying to me, both of you! Within
the hour I will be speaking with my lawyers.
Angèle (*tearfully*) Mother!
Laiguisier Do not cry, my dear. I shall arrange the separation,
everything.
Fauvinard My dear mother-in-law ——
Laiguisier Don't lie to me! I am not your dear, and I am no longer your
mother, in or out of law. Angèle, come with me!

Fauvinard If you'll allow me to explain ——
Laiguisier Don't lie to me! Come, Angèle!
Fauvinard But ——
Laiguisier Don't lie to me!

Laiguisier and Angèle go off through Entrance 2

Fauvinard My god! I'm ruined. What am I going to do?
Tardivaut My dear fellow, you must get a good lawyer.
Fauvinard What!
Tardivaut Your wife still loves you, I'm sure of it.

Fanchette enters through Entrance 1 with a card

Fanchette A gentleman called, monsieur. I told him you were having an
argument with your mother-in-law, but he said not to worry, he could
wait till it was over. (*Handing Fauvinard a card*) He gave me his card.
Shall I show him in?
Fauvinard Yes ... (*reading the card*) No! Wait! My God!
Tardivaut (*reading the card*) Monsieur de Bagnolles. Well, I must be
off.
Fauvinard (*clutching on to him*) No! No! For God's sake, stay with
me! I can't see him.
Tardivaut Why not?
Fauvinard Because he's seen me already at the Rue Saint-Lazare.
(*Indicating Entrance 3*) I'll go in there. You receive him.
Tardivaut What do I say?
Fauvinard Anything you like, only get rid of him.

Fauvinard goes off Entrance 3

Tardivaut You'd better show him in.
Fanchette Yes, monsieur.

Fanchette goes, Entrance 1

Tardivaut What do I say?

Bagnolles enters Entrance 1

Bagnolles Ah, monsieur ... Oh. The homeopath. Good-morning, doctor.
Tardivaut Eh? Oh, God, it's him!! Good-morning, monsieur.
Bagnolles I was wanting to talk to Counsellor Fauvinard. A matter of
some delicacy.

Tardivaut I see ...

Bagnolles I don't have the honour of knowing him, of course, but I understand he is representing my wife in a divorce case. Something happened last night which requires an explanation. If I could see him I am sure we could resolve the situation.

Tardivaut Yes. I'm sure. Unfortunately he is ... Very ill.

Bagnolles Oh, dear. It must be very sudden. He saw my wife only yesterday.

Tardivaut Yes. It happened only this morning. He'd been working all night. He had a seizure, after a dispute with his mother-in-law. I was called in. I'm a homeopath, you know.

Bagnolles Yes. I remember. Well, will you tell him not to take any action until I have seen him.

Tardivaut Not to worry. He won't be able to do anything. He's completely paralysed.

Bagnolles I'm sorry to hear it. Oh ... Doctor. A word.

Tardivaut Monsieur?

Bagnolles I'd be very much obliged if you didn't mention that you'd seen me last night.

Tardivaut Monsieur, you may rely upon my professional discretion.

Bagnolles Thank you, monsieur. You appear to have a very large practice ... For a homeopath.

Tardivaut Oh, it's huge.

Bagnolles Monsieur, your servant.

Tardivaut (*bowing*) Monsieur.

Bagnolles goes out Entrance 1

Tardivaut goes to Entrance 3

All right, you can come out now.

Fauvinard (*emerging*) He's gone?

Tardivaut He has!

Bagnolles enters from Entrance 1

Bagnolles I've just had a thought — my God! The other doctor!

Tardivaut (*to Fauvinard*) Say hello.

Fauvinard Monsieur. We meet again!

Bagnolles Both doctors. Counsellor Fauvinard's condition must be serious.

Fauvinard (*to Tardivaut*) What?

Tardivaut (*to Fauvinard*) I said you were ill.

Fauvinard Oh. (*To Bagnolles*) Yes. Very serious.

Tardivaut Very serious indeed.

Bagnolles Are you sure it's not possible to see him?

Fauvinard Absolutely impossible. He's out of his mind. He's very very ill.

Bagnolles Well, perhaps I could write him a note which you could give him. You see, the young lady to whom you were attending was an intimate acquaintance of mine, and subsequently, in the course of the evening, she was raided by the police. And some impudent scoundrel who happened to be caught there gave them my name instead of his, whatever it was.

Tardivaut Astonishing.

Fauvinard Words fail me.

Bagnolles It is a very grave situation, because the rogue made his escape, so the police came round to arrest me for not presenting myself to them at the police station after I had been caught — which I wasn't. So I avoided them and came here.

Fauvinard A very grave situation — Of course, I'm no legal expert, but ——

Tardivaut Sssh!

Bagnolles So you see, I desperately need Counsellor Fauvinard's good offices to persuade my wife Madame de Bagnolles to drop the charges.

Fauvinard Well ... (*Indicating Entrance 3 to Tardivaut and miming the turning of a key*)

Tardivaut Well, we'll see what we can do. If you would wait in there for a moment. (*Indicating Entrance 3*)

Bagnolles Very well, messieurs, I am in your hands. (*About to go in Entrance 3 he turns back, low to Fauvinard*) Oh ... doctor. A word. I'd be very much obliged if you didn't mention that you'd seen me last night.

Fauvinard Monsieur, you may rely upon my professional discretion.

Bagnolles (*about to go in Entrance 3, turning back again*) You know, it does seem a very odd coincidence to find you two doctors once again attending to someone I want to see.

Tardivaut
Fauvinard } (*together*) Yes ... Yes ... Extraordinary!

Gatinet puts his head round the door of Entrance 1

Gatinet Do I intrude?

Fauvinard Oh, my God! Uncle Gatinet!

Tardivaut Zizi's old man!

Bagnolles The bore who keeps falling asleep all the time! What's he doing here?

Gatinet (*approaching Fauvinard*) My dear Fauvinard!

Bagnolles What?

Fauvinard No, no! (*Low to Gatinet*) Shut up! I'm not Fauvinard. (*Loudly*) Fauvinard is ill.

Gatinet Eh? You're ill?

Fauvinard No, No! Not me! Fauvinard. (*Low to Gatinet*) Shut up!

Tardivaut (*to Bagnolles*) Pay no attention. He's a bit touched.

Bagnolles I noticed that yesterday.

Tardivaut (*low to Gatinet*) Shut up!

Gatinet My dear doctor. Delighted! (*Low to Tardivaut*) This is a little awkward, you know. I'd be very much obliged if you didn't mention that you'd seen me last night.

Tardivaut Monsieur, you may rely upon my professional discretion.

Gatinet (*low to Tardivaut*) I'm very grateful about what you did for Zizi, by the way. (*Seeing Bagnolles*) Ah, monsieur! We meet again!

Bagnolles Monsieur.

Gatinet (*nervously, coming up close to Bagnolles*) What a coincidence, eh?

Bagnolles Indeed!

Gatinet ⎱ (*together, low to each other*) I'd be very much obliged if
Bagnolles ⎰ you didn't mention ...

Gatinet Oh, I do beg your pardon!

Bagnolles Not at all. You were saying?

Gatinet I was just going to say that I'd be very much obliged if you didn't mention that you'd seen me last night.

Bagnolles Precisely what I was going to say myself.

Gatinet Oh, well! Splendid! Splendid! You may rely upon my discretion.

Bagnolles And you on mine, monsieur.

They shake hands

Now I must write to Counsellor Fauvinard.

Gatinet Eh? What do you mean? Write to ——

Tardivaut and Fauvinard come up on either side of him and carry him away from Bagnolles

Fauvinard ⎱
Tardivaut ⎰ (*together, low to Gatinet*) Shut up!

Fauvinard (*coming up to Bagnolles, indicating Entrance 3*) If you will come this way, I will find you the wherewithal.

Bagnolles (*as he goes off*) I am much obliged to you, doctor.

Bagnolles exits

Gatinet Eh? (*To Fauvinard*) Look here, what about my ten thousand
francs?
Fauvinard No time for that now! (*To Tardivaut*) Get rid of him! Just
get rid of him!

Fauvinard goes out via Entrance 3

Gatinet Where's he off to?
Tardivaut The law courts.
Gatinet (*about to follow Fauvinard into Entrance 3*) I must talk to him
about my money.
Tardivaut (*restraining him*) Later. Now, look here, I must go. I have ...
patients to see. Why don't you come with me?
Gatinet (*shaking him off*) No! (*Sitting*) I must have the money to give
to Zizi. She needs it for trombone lessons. She's expecting to see me
at midday.
Tardivaut (*shaking him, getting him to his feet*) No, no! You mustn't sit
down, you'll go to sleep!
Gatinet Oh, yes, of course. Now, doctor, what would you recommend
for this sleeping er ... thing.
Tardivaut Fresh air. Plenty of fresh air. Come along with me!
Gatinet I'll pay you for a consultation, you know ... (*Wandering towards
Entrance 3*) When I have the money.

Fauvinard comes out of Entrance 2, unseen by Gatinet

Fauvinard Oh, good grief! Hasn't he gone yet? Get rid of him! Just get
rid of him!
Tardivaut I've an idea.

Gatinet turns round

At the same time, Fauvinard exits Entrance 2

Gatinet Eh? Who was that?
Tardivaut Nothing! (*He moves towards the clock on the side table*) You
were saying. I'm listening.

*Gatinet wanders aimlessly about while Tardivaut adjusts the hands of
the clock. Tardivaut has to stop what he is doing whenever Gatinet looks
in his direction*

Gatinet You see I had two doctors. The first fellow, called Doctor ...
Something-or-other. I forget the name. I didn't have any confidence

in him. Quite a good doctor actually, but I didn't have any confidence in him. The second chap. Doctor — can't remember his name either, Doctor Something: but he was a splendid fellow. Rather expensive, but a brilliant doctor. He gave me some very good advice actually. He said, "number one: don't eat anything unhealthy; number two: don't drink anything that'll do you harm." First rate advice, that. Trouble was ...

Tardivaut What?

Gatinet I didn't take it.

Tardivaut Good heavens! Look at the time!

Gatinet Eh?

Tardivaut (*pointing at the clock*) Ten to twelve!

Gatinet (*staring at clock*) That can't be correct!

Tardivaut (*looking at his watch*) You're right, it isn't. It's five to twelve!

Gatinet (*looking at his watch*) My watch says ten-thirty.

Tardivaut It must have stopped.

A thought strikes Gatinet as he is holding his watch to his ear and puzzling over it

Gatinet Oh, Lord! Zizi is expecting me at twelve.

Tardivaut Is she?

Gatinet And if she doesn't see me, she'll have another attack of nerves. Like last night.

Tardivaut I'll come with you. I may be able to give her something which will calm her down.

Gatinet Oh, thank you, Doctor, you're like a father to her.

They go towards Entrance 1

Fanchette opens the door Entrance 1

Fanchette Oh! Where's monsieur?

Gatinet Gone to the law courts! Come on, Doctor! We haven't a moment to lose!

Gatinet goes off Entrance 1

Fanchette Gone to the law courts?

Tardivaut Pay no attention. (*Indicating Entrance 3*) He's in there.

Gatinet (*off*) Come on, Doctor!

Tardivaut goes off Entrance 1

Fanchette Doctor? What's going on?

Fauvinard enters Entrance 2 not seeing Fanchette

Fauvinard Ah, Gatinet's gone, has he? (*He goes to Entrance 3*)
Fanchette Monsieur!
Fauvinard (*turning and seeing her*) What? Yes! What is it?
Fanchette It's the lady from yesterday. Your client. She's waiting in the salon.
Fauvinard Madame de Bagnolles! And her husband's here. I can't possibly see her at the moment.
Fanchette Shall I tell her, monsieur?
Fauvinard No, no! I'll go and see her ... And tell her that I can't see her.

Fauvinard goes off Entrance 1

Fanchette What's wrong with everyone?

Laiguisier enters through Entrance 2

Laiguisier Where is he?
Fanchette He's in the salon, madame, with his client. A very attractive lady, madame.
Laiguisier The one he was with yesterday evening, eh?
Fanchette Yes, madame.
Laiguisier I thought so! His mistress! Well, we're going to catch him red-handed this time. He's bound to come back in here with her. I shall conceal myself. You may go, Fanchette!
Fanchette Yes, madame.

Fanchette exits through Entrance 1, shaking her head

Laiguisier Now where? (*Considering Entrance 3*) No! Here!

Laiguisier goes to hide behind Entrance 2

Bagnolles enters from Entrance 3, carrying a letter

Bagnolles Nobody here! Very odd house, this. He must get this letter. Oh, well! (*He drops the letter on the desk, goes to Entrance 1, opens the door and looks out*) My God! My wife! And the doctor! (*He rushes back into the room and dives down behind the sofa*)

Laiguisier opens the door to Entrance 2 so that it is ajar

Just as she does, Mme de B enters, carrying a sheaf of papers, followed by Fauvinard

Mme de B No more than five minutes. I promise you, monsieur, but it is vital.
Fauvinard Very well, madame. Please be seated.

Mme de B sits on the chair opposite the desk

Fauvinard goes to Entrance 3, locks the door and pockets the key

Ah! Locked in. That's better.
Mme de B Monsieur?
Fauvinard You have my undivided attention, madame!
Mme de B I have all the documents here relating to my husband's extravagances. Would you care to look them over?
Bagnolles (*aside, from behind the sofa*) Look them over! The doctor?
Laiguisier (*aside, from behind the door*) She really is his client!
Fauvinard Madame, I am beginning to wonder whether I should take this case.
Mme de B But, monsieur, you have been so eloquent, so persuasive. Why are you hesitating? I beg you, Monsieur Fauvinard ——
Bagnolles (*aside, from behind the sofa*) My God! It's Fauvinard!
Fauvinard Certainly, madame, you have an excellent case. Monsieur de Bagnolles' conduct has been utterly deplorable.
Bagnolles (*aside, from behind the sofa*) What!
Fauvinard (*seeing Bagnolles, nearly falling off his chair*) Good grief! It's him!
Mme de B Are you all right, monsieur?
Fauvinard Yes. Fine. I'm just a little er ... (*He has a fit of coughing*)
Mme de B You were saying that Monsieur de Bagnolles' conduct has been utterly deplorable
Fauvinard Madame, if you will allow me to explain ——
Mme de B It is true that I hesitated at first. The fear of a scandal ——
Fauvinard And how right you were, madame ——
Mme de B But you have persuaded me. I hesitate no longer. We will make him suffer the full rigour of the law.
Fauvinard But, madame, I believe you may be mistaken ——
Laiguisier (*from behind the door*) Pah! Ridiculous man!
Fauvinard (*seeing Laiguisier, nearly falling off his chair*) Good grief! Her too!

Mme de B Is anything the matter, monsieur?
Fauvinard No, no. Fine!
Mme de B You were saying that I might be mistaken?
Fauvinard Perhaps, madame. Having considered all the possibilities ——
Mme de B Are you by any chance proposing to mount a defence of faithless husbands?

Bagnolles raises his head from behind the sofa and, unseen by Mme de B, nods at Fauvinard

Fauvinard (*hesitating*) Well ... Why not?
Bagnolles (*from behind the sofa*) That's my boy!
Laiguisier (*from behind the door*) This is monstrous!
Fauvinard (*rising from his chair, to himself*) I've burnt my boats. Here goes. (*To Mme de B*) Madame, listen to me!
Mme de B (*stony-faced*) I am listening, Monsieur Fauvinard. In some amazement.
Fauvinard I say to you, madame, that a wife may very often have cause to demand a separation from her husband. But it is a grave matter, madame, and not to be entered into lightly, or foolishly, or ——
Mme de B Certainly not! How dare you suggest ——
Fauvinard Madame! Please allow me to finish! Believe me, your cause is mine.
Mme de B It doesn't appear to be, monsieur.
Fauvinard On the contrary, madame, if I were to plead your case, I would get your separation for you. It would be so simple. How easy it would be to prove this man's guilt. (*Indicating Bagnolles*)

Mme de B looks behind her. Bagnolles ducks down behind the sofa

(*Loudly*) But!

Mme de B looks back at Fauvinard

Have we truly read this man's heart? Have we paused to reflect upon what forced him upon a path that he now bitterly regrets? Yes, we may have deserted the conjugal hearth. Yes, we may have gone in search of forbidden fruit. But whose fault is that? Is it really ours and ours alone? (*In Laiguisier's direction*) Has not this unhappy man a mother-in-law who has made his wife — er ... life quite unbearable?
Laiguisier (*from behind the door*) This is monstrous! What is he saying?
Mme de B (*flatly*) No he hasn't.

Fauvinard I beg your pardon?

Mme de B He hasn't got a mother-in-law. My mother died when I was three.

Fauvinard Ah ... (*Recovering his eloquence*) That may be so, madame, but it will not prevent a lawyer from affirming that he has a mother-in-law and what is said in a court of law, true or false, remains the truth for all time. After all, every woman must at one time have had a mother — that is indisputable, you have yourself admitted it — and so it follows that every married man has had a mother-in-law, alive or dead. That is the higher truth to which all lawyers pledge themselves when they dedicate their lives to the cause of Justice. Consequently, madame, what judge is there living who would not find a great treasure house of compassion in his heart for a man so unfortunately oppressed. A man who loved his wife — because assuredly he did love her! — who had no happiness or joy except from her, but whom the tyrannies, the annoyances, the continual suspicions of a mother-in-law drove him from his house ... exiled him from the conjugal home ... Launched him into the pit of folly, into the adventures of an existence that dare not speak its name! ... And it is this man that you would wish to reduce to desperation! ... It is this man whom you would reject, even were he to return repentant, chastened, (*holding his bandaged hand*) savaged by life's horrors? And begging humbly on his knees for forgiveness. But you could not reject him ... (*Turning to Laiguisier*) No, you could not be so heartless ... (*To Mme de B*) Because he loves you still ... And you still love him. Don't you?

Mme de B It's true.

Laiguisier (*holding a handkerchief to her eye*) I am moved. Reluctantly, I admit, I am moved.

Bagnolles (*still behind the sofa*) Well done, monsieur!

Laiguisier He certainly possesses the eloquence necessary for a successful legal career.

Fauvinard Open your arms to him, madame! Forgive and forget! Let us have no talk of separation! Let us talk rather of reconciliation. (*To Bagnolles*) Is that not what you came here for, monsieur? Monsieur?

Bagnolles (*emerging from behind the sofa*) Berthe!

Mme de B (*running to him*) Henri!

Bagnolles and Mme de B embrace

Laiguisier (*emerging from behind the door*) Son-in-law, you may embrace me!

Fauvinard (*submitting to the embrace*) Oh, good grief!

Angèle enters

Angèle Mother! What are you doing?
Laiguisier Angèle, embrace your husband.
Angèle But Mother —— !
Laiguisier Angèle, will you for once in your life, do as you're told!
Angèle Yes, Mother. (*She embraces Fauvinard*)
Laiguisier If only you knew how this man has made me weep.
Angèle What!
Laiguisier With admiration, child! With admiration!
Fauvinard At last! I've won my first case.

Fanchette enters

Fanchette It's Monsieur Gatinet.
Fauvinard Oh, grief!

The others groan

Show him in!
Fanchette He's crying like a baby.

Gatinet enters weeping

Fauvinard That will be all, Jacques!

Fanchette exits

Gatinet I have come to say goodbye.
Fauvinard You're leaving!
Gatinet She showed me the door, you know. My Zizi. (*He points to Fauvinard*) And all because of you!
Laiguisier What's this!
Gatinet All because you wouldn't let me have a miserable ten thousand francs.
Fauvinard Well, there you are, you see! She only wanted you for my money.
Gatinet But that's only fair. I only wanted her for ——
Fauvinard Yes, well we won't go into that now. You've learned your lesson. Once bitten, twice shy.

Tardivaut enters

Laiguisier I think we have all been bitten.

Gatinet Anyway, the doctor has recommended that I go away and get some fresh country air. Where is the doctor? (*Seeing Tardivaut*) Ah, there you are, doctor!

Laiguisier Doctor! You are no doctor, monsieur!

Fauvinard (*low to Tardivaut*) Everything's been resolved, my friend.

Bagnolles What's this? You're not a doctor?

Tardivaut I admit it freely, monsieur. I am not a doctor. Not even a homeopath.

Gatinet I don't understand.

Bagnolles Well, if you're not a doctor, what are you?

Tardivaut I'm a lawyer, of course.

Bagnolles I should have known!

Gatinet I don't understand! If you're ——

Tardivaut Which reminds me. I have news. In the early hours of this morning Madame Césarine left Paris.

Bagnolles Oh, God!

Mme de B What?

Bagnolles Nothing, my dear!

Fauvinard Why?

Tardivaut The police were wanting to question her. Something to do with the Veauradieux Case.

Laiguisier The Veauradieux Case! I knew it!

Gatinet I too will be happy to leave Paris, madame, if you will accompany me.

Laiguisier Oh, don't be absurd!

Gatinet My God, you're a fine figure of a woman! Just like my mother!

Fauvinard And I shall leave Paris too. Angèle, you have always wanted us to go into the country. We shall go there and I shall become a Justice of the Peace.

Angèle Oh, Armand! You'd give up all this? For me?

Fauvinard Gladly, my love!

Angèle and Fauvinard embrace

Laiguisier You most certainly will not! It is quite clear to me that you have an extremely promising and lucrative career ahead of you as an advocate in the divorce courts. You give that up over my dead body!

Fauvinard Don't tempt me, madame.

Gatinet Wait a minute! I still don't understand! (*To Tardivaut*) If you're not a doctor, a homeo —— whatever it is, what were you doing with my Zizi up there in the er ——

Fauvinard Oh, be quiet!

Tardivaut Sit down!
Bagnolles Go to sleep!
Fauvinard Sit down!
Gatinet No, I will not sit down!
Tardivaut   ⎫
Fauvinard   ⎬ (*together*) SIT DOWN!
Bagnolles   ⎭

The three men push him down on to the sofa. He sleeps

Laiguisier Peace at last!

Fauvinard embraces Angèle, Bagnolles embraces Madame de Bagnolles,
Tardivaut kisses Laiguisier's hand. Gatinet snores

Quickish fade

C<small>URTAIN</small>

FURNITURE AND PROPERTY LIST

ACT I

On stage: Desk. *On it*: documents, legal tomes, writing paper, pen,
envelopes, stamps
Two chairs
Sofa
Side table. *On it*: clock

Off stage: Letter (**Fanchette**)
Letter (**Fanchette**)

Personal: **Tardivaut**: bill (in pocket), watch
Laiguisier: corsage

ACT II

On stage: Chaise-longue
Upright piano. *On it*: lamp
Easel with framed picture of black poodle
Largish round table with heavy velvet tablecloth. *On it*:
pack of cards
Small escritoire with drawer containing smelling salts
Armchair
Key in lock of door (Entrance 2)

Off stage: Letter (**Césarine**)
Extravagant bouquet of red roses (**Tardivaut**)
Bloodstained handkerchief (**Tardivaut**)
Vase of water (**Sophie**)
Bloodstained handkerchief (**Thérèse**)
Bandage (**Tardivaut**)
Bloodstained handkerchief, corpse of black poodle (**Fauvinard**)
Umbrella, bag containing crumpled piece of paper (**Laiguisier**)
Brown paper (**Thérèse**)

Personal: **Césarine**: hand mirror
Fauvinard: coins, handkerchief (in pockets)
Césarine: showy ring

ACT III

On stage: As ACT I

Off stage: Bundle including tablecloth (**Fauvinard**)
Brown paper parcel containing **Fauvinard**'s coat and
   trousers (**Laiguisier**)
Card (**Fanchette**)
Letter (**Bagnolles**)
Sheaf of papers (**Mme de B**)

Personal: **Gatinet**: watch
Laiguisier: handkerchief

LIGHTING PLOT

Property fittings required: lamp

ACT I

To open: General interior lighting

Cue 1	**Laiguisier**: "Eleven Rue Saint-Lazare!" *Quick fade to black-out*	(Page 27)

ACT II

To open: General interior lighting

Cue 2	**Thérèse**: "Revenge!" *Quickish fade*	(Page 60)

ACT III

To open: General interior lighting

Cue 3	**Gatinet** snores *Quickish fade*	(Page 79)

EFFECTS PLOT

ACT I

Cue 1   **Fauvinard** goes off Entrance 3   (Page 9)
Sound of front door slamming

ACT II

Cue 2   To open ACT II   (Page 28)
Barking of a small, aggressive dog

Cue 3   **Césarine**: "... I'm sure about the bad luck."   (Page 30)
Doorbell rings

Cue 4   **Césarine** opens the door of Entrance 2   (Page 30)
Torrent of barking

Cue 5   **Césarine** shuts the door   (Page 30)
Barking subsides

Cue 6   **Fauvinard**: "From all sides ..."   (Page 32)
Sound of frenzied barking

Cue 7   **Césarine**: "Naughty Niniche!"   (Page 33)
A yap

Cue 8   **Sophie** opens the door of Entrance 2   (Page 33)
A torrent of aggressive barks and growls

Cue 9   **Fauvinard** goes to Entrance 2   (Page 34)
Sound of yapping and growling

Cue 10   **Fauvinard** goes to Entrance 2 and listens   (Page 35)
Loud burst of growling and barking

Cue 11   **Thérèse**: "Let me out! Let me out!"   (Page 35)
Further yapping and growling

Cue 12   **Fauvinard**: "Very well!"   (Page 35)
Further outburst of yapping and growling